Mary English ˅
Switzerland at   f
Zurich. She is ˸   private
practice in the ˗˗˗
She is a member of The Astrological Association of Great
Britain and the author of more than 15 non-fiction titles.

*"Mary English has a heavenly approach to love
through the stars. Gently, she guides you into the
subtle art of astrology with romantic poetry.
Mary leads you on a journey where you gain deep
insight into yourself as a lover and your potential
soul mate."*

Robert Currey, Astrologer & Founder of Equinox

The Astrology of Lovers

How Astrology Can
Help You Love Better
A Practical Guide

Also by Mary English

Published by Hensley Healing Publishing
6 Easy Steps in Astrology
*The Astrology of Indigos, Everyday Solutions to
Spiritual Difficulties*

Published by John Hunt Publishing
How to Survive a Pisces
How to Bond with an Aquarius
How to Cheer up a Capricorn
How to Believe in a Sagittarius
How to Win the Trust of a Scorpio
How to Love a Libra
How to Soothe a Virgo
How to Lavish a Leo
How to Care for a Cancer
How to Listen to a Gemini
How to Satisfy a Taurus
How to Appreciate an Aries

A Little at a Time,
Homeopathy For You and Those You Love

The Astrology of Lovers

How Astrology Can
Help You Love Better
A Practical Guide

Mary English

Hensley Healing Publishers
Bath, UK

First published by Hensley Healing Publishers, 2017
Bath, UK

Copyright: Mary English 2017

ISBN: **978-1542972987**

All rights reserved. Except for brief quotations in
critical articles or reviews, no part of this book may
be reproduced in any manner without prior written
permission from the publishers.

The rights of Mary English as author have been
asserted in accordance with the Copyright, Designs
and Patents Act 1988 UK.

Cover Design: David T.J. Powell

Astrological charts with kind permission of Alois at
www.astro.com and www.astrodatabank.com

CONTENTS

Astrological Charts List

This book is dedicated to those I have loved over the years, from my first love, to my first husband to my current soul mate and to all those in between

Your Love Has Meant a Lot to Me.
You Have Been and Are My Greatest Teachers.

Acknowledgements

I would like to thank the thousands of clients I have worked with since I began working with divination in my teens.

I would also like to thank these wonderful people for supporting my writing journey and willingly and lovingly agreeing to read through, critique and feedback to me: Mandy Andrews, Jill Trelease, Neharika Gupta, Lucy-Sian Clark, Sandie Sedgbeer, Mr T, Julie Lee, Bella Doe, Niki Mclynn, Alam Octinur, Denise Solomon and Анастасия Wickins.

Jennifer Fuson for urging me to publish this time.

Elizabeth Rose for her generosity.

All the members of the Bath Writers Group, in particular Kay Leitch and Celia Gunn.

David T.J. Powell for his beautiful cover design.

Introduction

Astrology has existed for more than 2,000 years and is used in lots of different ways in almost every country in the world. It's a truly international language.

I didn't know much about Astrology when I started dating in my teens and got married in my late twenties. I knew I was a Pisces, with something somewhere in Gemini but that was about it.

After my Gemini ex-husband and I divorced and after my Homeopath mentioned about my 'Saturn Return', I threw myself into the subject to find out 'why-it-had-gone-wrong' and also what I could do to improve my love life and make better choices.

On the long journey to understand Astrology, I also learned heaps about myself, which was enlightening. I now understand my Love Needs and how to make sure they are satisfied. I re-married when I was in my early 40s to someone far more compatible with me.

However, that first marriage had a lot of compatibility and exploring the Astrology of it gave me a better understanding of why it ended when it did. The extra plus point was we have a lovely son, to whom my How to Love a Libra book is dedicated.

Understanding your 'self' can be a full-time job if your chart is complex and having some pointers on the way will give you the confidence to live a more fulfilling life.

I am a professional Astrologer with over 20 years of private practice. I see clients, make charts, work out solutions and give encouragement to my clients to help them back on their Life Path.

The *most* asked question in my practice is about people's love lives. So after nagging myself since 2013 to write a book to help them, I've eventually finished this work. It took far longer than I thought it would and hopefully it was worth waiting for.

This book will not only give you the Astrological explanations for your love life, and how to attract what you'd like for a lover but also how to mend or repair or improve the relationship that you're in at the moment.
I do hope you enjoy reading it.

What is Love and a Lover?
The title of this book is The Astrology of Lovers, so we will have to explore exactly what a lover is, and also what love is, as without love, you can't be a lover.

So, what is a lover? My dictionary defines it as:

 'A person in love with another.'

Sounds simple, doesn't it?

But then that raises the age-old question: 'What is love anyway?'
Back to the dictionary again:

'Love *noun* deep affection or fondness for person or thing; sexual passion, sexual relations.'

I don't agree totally with the second part. It's perfectly possible to love someone or something *without* having any sexual feelings for them or it.

The love of a baby by its parents isn't (normally) sexual. Equally the love of an animal, say a pet, doesn't involve sexual feelings, so I think for the purposes of defining what love is, for the purposes of this book, we shall leave it at the first explanation.

Deep Affection or Fondness for a Person

And what does my trusty dictionary define a lover as:

'Lover *noun* person (esp. man) in love with another; man with whom woman is having sexual relations; (in pl) pair in love.'

Well, that didn't quite hit it for me either! Why does a lover have to be a man? Whyever can't it be a woman? Either my dictionary is terribly out-of-date or the people who wrote and edited it... were blokes.

So a lover is a person who you can have deep affections for.
Deep fondness etc.
Or a lover could be a person who has deep affections for you.
It works both ways.
The other thing I might disagree with (in my personal opinion) is that I don't think the thing that love is, is a noun. I'd be more inclined, in my personal opinion to think of it like being a verb.
Something that you 'do' rather than own.
A lover is definitely a noun. As a noun is a Person, Place or Thing.
But is love a thing?
Can you see it? No.
Can you hold it? No.
Does it have a colour or texture or smell or taste? No again.

How can love be a thing?
It can't.
It's something you feel: an emotion.
And it comes in lots of different guises.
You can love your football team as much as you love your wife.

You could also love your husband or boyfriend as much or more than you love to play the piano.
Everything is relative.
Love can be so hard to describe, let alone quantify, which is why I've used as my chart examples two rather famous lovers who were also poets. And two others, one of whom was a famous musician and his wife, a creative artist. As in my experience, poets and creative people are very good at expressing love and loving in ways most of us would never even think of.

XLIII

How do I love thee? Let me count the ways.
I love thee to the depth and breadth and height
My soul can reach, when feeling out of sight
For the ends of Being and ideal Grace.
I love thee to the level of every day's
Most quiet need, by sun and candlelight.
I love thee freely, as men strive for Right;
I love thee purely, as they turn from Praise.
I love thee with the passion put to use
In my old griefs, and with my childhood's faith.
I love thee with a love I seemed to lose
With my lost saints, --- I love thee with the breath,
Smiles, tears, of all my life! --- and, if God choose,
I shall but love thee better after death.

Elizabeth Barrett Browning. Penultimate verse from
Sonnets from the Portuguese 1850

—

And now .. I will not say a word, my love of loves, my dearest, dearest Ba, - not one word - but I will go out and walk where I can be alone, and think out all my thought of you, and bless you and love you with nothing to intercept the blessing and the love. I will look in the direction of London and send my heart there . . Dear, dear love, I kiss you and commend you to God.

Robert letter to Elizabeth postmark May 2, 1846 from *The Love Letters of Robert Browning & Elizabeth Barrett* Edited by V.E. Stack

---People used to say to me, 'You expect too much - you are too romantic.' And my answer always was that 'I could not expect too much when I expected nothing at all' .. which was the truth - for I never thought (and how often I have said that!) I never thought that anyone whom I could love, would stoop to love me .. the two things seemed clearly incompatible to my understanding.

Elizabeth letter to Robert postmark December 24,1845 From *The Love Letters of Robert Browning & Elizabeth Barrett* Edited by V.E. Stack

If someone thinks that love and peace is a cliché that must have been left behind in the Sixties, that's his problem. Love and peace are eternal.

John Lennon

It is very difficult for us to know we love somebody because it is an insecure position to be in. But in the end, it is important to be honest about your love because life is not that long.

Yoko Ono

Astrological Glossary

AC: Stands for Ascendant, the moment of your birth.

Aspect: The mathematical relationship between two planets in a chart. How many degrees apart.
The Aspects that we're using in this book are:
Conjunction: When two planets are in the same sign and very near to each other, to a maximum of 8 degrees. Any further than that and they're out of orb.

Opposition: When two planets are directly opposite each other.

Square: When two planets are 90 degrees apart but in the same Modality or Mode so Pisces is Square Sagittarius but they're both Mutable signs.

Trine: When two planets are 120 degrees apart but in the same Element. So it unites the Water, Fire, Earth or Air signs.

MC: Stands for Medium Coeli, the highest point on the ecliptic, the path the Sun seems to take around the Earth (when in fact it's the Earth that is circling around the Sun.)

Modes or Modality: Fixed, Cardinal and Mutable
Fixed: Taurus, Leo, Scorpio, Aquarius live in the present and don't like change.
Cardinal: Aries, Cancer, Libra, Capricorn like to think about the future and to organise things.
Mutable: Gemini, Virgo, Sagittarius, Pisces like to think about the past a lot and love change.

Orb: The allowance of how far apart an aspect can be.
Upsetment: A state of being upset. A Mary Word!

Chapter One

Using Astrology To Learn About Yourself

Most clients I meet are either hoping to be in a relationship or complaining about the one they are in.

I think it is part of being human, that the grass always looks greener on the other side.

One thing I learned really quickly was how Astrology can help us make good life choices, once we understand ourselves through our own chart.

I could give you succinct advice on 'how to attract your soul-mate' but what would be the point if you hate yourself and all your past relationships have self-destructed?

First, we have to learn about ourselves, before we can even hope to have a good relationship with anyone. What we will be learning in this chapter is 'how' we need to be loved. What our love needs are.

What to look for in your chart

I will assume at this point, that you've read one of my books on your own Sun sign, which describes how to make your own birth chart, using the free on-line resource www.astro.com

We learned in each book what Sun sign, Ascendant and Moon you have, so that information I won't go into too much detail here.

Those parts of a chart are THE most important and you need to keep them in mind when you're determining your own love needs.

Yes, the planets Venus and Mars are important in helping you understand what your love needs are, but if we ignore the crucial parts of your 'self' we'll never come to an understanding of your needs.
And it's your emotional needs that have to be fulfilled, or you'll never truly feel happy in any relationship.

Zodiac

I have a very elderly Astrological computer programme called Zodiac that runs on Windows 95 (I now use a Mac so I have to use more software to run it) that allows me to calculate how compatible I am with someone else.
It rates it out of 100%. 100% being high and very compatible, 0% being very low and incompatible.
It also will let me rate my own compatibility with myself, not that there are two parts of me, but if I line up my own chart with another one exactly the same, it gives me that percentage out of 100%
So, if I were to meet someone who was the exact same as myself, how would we get along?
I rate 70% with myself.
It's a weird feeling knowing I wouldn't be 100% compatible with someone identical with me! This is the work we need to do *before* we work out what we're looking for in a relationship, or how to improve the one that we're in. Unless we acknowledge, and understand our own failings or attributes, all relationships will be tricky.

However, if you *haven't* read my book for your Sun sign (naughty you!), here is a quick run down of what you need to do and know.

Chart of the Heavens

Planet: A celestial body that orbits around the Sun. Star: With the exception of the Moon and the planets from Mercury to Pluto, every fixed point of light in the sky is a star, including the Sun. However, in Astrology we use the term 'planet' for all of them. So if you catch me calling the Sun a planet, that is an astrological term, not one used in astronomy. Astronomers don't call the Moon a planet they call it a 'satellite' or 'celestial body'. Sounds rather dull to me! However, sometimes Astrologers call the Sun (which is technically a star) and the Moon 'Lights' or 'Luminaries': Natural Light-Giving Bodies. I like that far better.

If you imagine that the centre of your Astrological chart is the earth, the map is made up of where each planet was, in each segment of the sky, in relation to your place and time of birth.
We use a circle to plot their positions, which is now made easier by using computer programmes that use astronomical information. When Astrology was developed by the Babylonians, over 2,000 years ago the movements and placements of the planets were made by educated men. Later the information was kept in a book called an Ephemeris. Nowadays, all you need to do is use a good computer programme or the wonderful Swiss resource www.astro.com

Each chart includes the 10 planets: the Sun, the Moon, Mercury, Venus, Mars, Jupiter, Saturn, Uranus, Neptune and Pluto and each planet represents a different area of life.

The most important parts of a chart are the Ascendant, the sign and location of the Sun and the sign of the Moon.

—
9

The Ascendant
How you came into the world
The Ascendant is determined by the actual time of birth, so you need to know the accurate time to get the correct Ascendant because it changes sign every two hours. So someone born at 10am will have a different Ascendant from someone born at 12pm. In Astrology we classify the Ascendant as being the ouside part of you, the bit people meet first. The image we want people to see, in fact the image people *will* see.

Your Ascendant is what you display at a party, or to your parents, or when you're under pressure. It's the coat you wear, the glasses you see the world through, how you viewed the world when you came into it.

Your beginning.

As you were being born, *the* most important part of your chart was in a sign signifying how you 'came into the world'. It could be in the sign of Virgo making you discriminating, analytical and prone to wanting to categorise things. Or it could be in the sign of Cancer, wanting to 'feel at home', loving Mum, wanting protection and financial security.

Each Ascendant sign has a different meaning and will modify the sign of your Sun sign.

The Sun
Rules who you are

The Sun represents who you are. The ego. That which identifies you. Most people know what Sun sign they are, even if they don't know anything else about Astrology. In a birth chart the sign and location of the Sun describes how you will approach life. Will you be fearless or timid, creative or shy? It also describes what you will find interesting and how you will express your personality. Most people know what Sun sign they are, even if they don't know much about Astrology and it's a good place to start. Your Sun sign represents your motivations and interests.

The Moon
Rules the emotions and instincts

The Moon in Astrology represents how we feel about things. If the Sun is who we are, and the Ascendant is how we project ourselves, then the Moon is how we respond emotionally to things.

In Astronomy the Moon reflects the light of the Sun, and we view the Moon in a similar way in Astrology. We say that the Moon represents how we feel. Not who we are. You could say that the Sun is a masculine planet and the Moon is a female one as the Sun is more go-getting and the Moon is softer and more reflective, less aggressive.

The Moon changes sign every two days or so as there are 12 signs of the Zodiac and it takes the Moon approximately 28 days to travel through all the signs and make a complete orbit of our Earth.

The Elements
Our energy levels

The signs of the (western) Zodiac can be divided into Fire, Earth, Air and Water.
The Fire signs are: Aries, Leo and Sagittarius.
The Earth signs are Taurus, Virgo and Capricorn.
The Air signs are: Gemini, Libra and Aquarius.
The Water signs are: Cancer, Scorpio and Pisces.

It is useful to think of the elements when you are considering your chart.
If you are a Fire sign you will travel faster emotionally than others, when it come to your love life.

At the other end of the scale are the Earth signs, who prefer their love life to progress much more slowly. I like to think of the Elements as being different speeds that each sign travels. Aries is the fastest sign and travels at 100mph.
Taurus is the slowest sign and travels at a happy, legal 30mph and the other signs fit in between.
Fire signs always want to 'do' stuff NOW, while Earth signs need time to assimilate information and feelings.
Air signs question everything! So their speed is faster than Earth but not as fast as Fire. They want answers, but they want to debate and talk and think and review what they've thought and said and what their partner/friend/family member said or thought. Not that anyone can ever know what someone else is thinking and I'm always amazed at how many Air signs ask me what I think their partner/friend/family member might be or could be thinking.
Who knows?

Air-sign speed is fast-ish and they accelerate really quickly and can just as quickly decelerate while they think themselves into complex places.

Water signs are mid-speed. Not as slow as Earth or even as fast as Air. And I imagine their speed as fluctuating. One day they're zooming along at 50mph, just below the speed limit, then later in the day they slow down to 35mph and every now and then suddenly brake and need to ask themselves (or others) how they're feeling.

The Main Parts of Your Chart

At the moment we are going to make it easier for you to understand your love life Astrologically, by focusing only on the main parts of your chart.
In a further chapter I will discuss more complex astrological love–life information.

If you know the sign of your Ascendant, then working out how you approach and get to know potential partners is much easier.

Fire sign Ascendants will want any new relationship to progress quickly.
Meet today.
Date tomorrow.
Plan the wedding.

Air sign Ascendants will want to move reasonably quickly, however they will want to discuss, weigh-up, talk about, plan, think and think some more.
If your Ascendant is in an Air sign, you will approach all relationships with a questioning mind.

A Water sign Ascendant will need to work out how they feel about any new relationship. They will need time and space to process any emotions that come up.

If this is your Ascendant sign, then allow yourself *plenty* of time to let your *feelings* catch up. Don't rush yourself. Allow all those feelings to surface, greet them and make friends with them. Keep the tissues handy. Water signs are good at crying!

An Earth sign Ascendant won't be rushed. So please don't try. If this is you, give yourself lots and lots and lots of time. Oodles of it! Plan things carefully. Work out prices (the Earth signs are more tuned-into how much things cost=practical considerations). Discuss dates. Stick to them. Plan carefully. Take each day at a time.

The same advice applies to your Sun and Moon signs. Once you've discovered them, you will then understand how we need to take into account all the different parts of your psyche.

Maybe you've got a fast-moving Ascendant wanting it all to happen NOW, but your Sun sign is a feely Water sign, gripping the tissue-box and weeping into your pillow at night, while your Moon sign is an Air sign wanting ANSWERS and EXPLANATIONS and REASONS (this is my experience of my own chart).

If you don't know your Ascendant, because you don't know your time of birth, you can still use Astrology. You'll know your Sun, Moon and planets signs, which are just as important as anything else. However you won't know what order your chart is in.

Madly in Love Compared to
Deeply in Love

A word of warning.
I've worked with far too many people with this problem and I know it happens a lot.
If you've found the birth data for someone you're 'madly in love with'... just keep that information to yourself.

It doesn't matter how wonderful their chart looks to you. If you haven't ever dated them or they're not actually exhibiting romantic actions in your direction, then their chart is meaningless.

Being madly in love, is madness.

Being deeply in love isn't madness. It's natural.

If loving someone keeps you awake at night, makes you want to phone/text/message talk about them all the time, that's a mental health issue, not love.

If you 'think' you're 100% compatible with someone but they're 'getting over a previous relationship' or 'too shy to ask you out' or 'deeply hurt from past loves' then they're certainly not going to date you just because you like them.

Rather than looking at their chart, look at your own.

Maybe you've got Saturn transiting your Venus or Uranus conjuncting your Moon.

There will be an Astrological explanation for what's happening now, but that doesn't mean this other person is feeling the same way about you...

Watch out for transits that involve Pluto, as then the feelings will be desperate/anguished/painful and/or dire.
Distance yourself from the other person until the transit is a little less acute and re-evaluate.

Chart Shape

When you make your first chart all you will see is an enormous amount of squiggles, lots of lines and maybe colours and you can very easily get overwhelmed.
Keep things as easy as possible and for that first look, just concentrate on what shape your chart makes.

The house system I use is called Equal House. It's the easiest to learn and one of the oldest. Most websites will use a default system called Placidus, which makes any chart look very uneven. Always use Equal House if you want to study chart shape.
www.astro.com does give you that option in their 'Extended Chart Selection' which is filed under Free Horoscopes/Chart Drawings & Calculations.
The box to click is called House System in the Options section of the page.

Looking at the shape of a Birth-chart is a simple way to understand 'the whole person'. There are 7 major types of shapes and each Birth-chart will fit into one. Do not make the mistake of applying these shapes in a rigid manner i.e. 'Everyone with a splash chart will find it difficult to specialise or concentrate'. There are no 'fixed expressions' in Astrology, just the same as we are all capable of change.
These shapes were first written about by chap called Marc Edmund Jones, an American Astrologer, in 1941.[1]

I find them extremely useful in making an analysis of the energies in a birth chart and wrote about Cluster, Bowl and Bundle charts in my book *The Astrology of Indigos, Everyday Solutions to Spiritual Difficulties*.[2]

Just looking at the shapes the charts make can give you a flavour of and idea of, how the energies are within that person. They represent an aspect of the 'self' in a pictorial form. My chart might be splashed. Yours might be bundled. You might notice that I have a finger in every pie while you are focused and happiest when you do one thing at a time.

Observing how someone is, and what they do in certain circumstances helps us understand that person a bit more. Looking at and marveling at the differences between each chart shape unique to us makes Astrology more than just a set of numbers or names. Shape and form come into it.

If you imagine that a birth chart is a representation of your life's energies, then those energies will need expression somehow and your chart shape is a little like your fingerprints or your eye colour. It's never going to change.

I think of a person's chart shape as their personal energies and how they express them in their world that they live in. Well, the world they *think* they live in, nothing can ultimately be proved.

The Splash
With the Splash the planets are all around the circle, nothing in one place, 10 planets evenly distributed throughout the 12 houses.

At its worst, this type of Chart indicates a person whose energies are 'scattered'. At its best, it means a capacity for a genuine universal interest, and a gift for bringing order, where there is chaos.

The Splay
This has an irregular distribution of planets around the circle. This represents an intense personality who cannot be limited to any particular point of application. Splash's energy is even, Splay's is uneven. They work best when they can divide their time and energy between lots of different 'projects', feeling involved and included. The downside is they can't focus on any one task and (on a bad day) will waste time just 'pottering' around.

The Locomotive
This is similar in shape to the See Saw but the opposite elements aren't directly opposite to each other. They're sort of sideways on.

This type is motivated more by external factors in the environment, than by aspects of their own character. The planets are clustered into 3 houses, balanced against the remaining planets in 5 houses. They have 3 empty houses, next door to each other. With a self-driving individuality, this shape exhibits a dynamic and exceptionally practical capacity, which is neither broad like the Splash, nor obsessive like the Bundle.

An eccentric balance.

The Seesaw

This shape has 2 opposite 8, or 3 opposite 7 or 4 opposite 6 and so on...

It ideally will have two symmetrically opposite segments at least 3 houses apart.

The Seesaw temperament lives in a world of conflicts, of definite polarities. These people work best when they divide their time between the two segments of the chart. They need variety and change. I always recommend clients with this chart shape divide their time between two life projects. Maybe home and work. Or two hobbies. They're not happy doing the same thing everyday. Equally, they're unhappy changing too much. They can swing one way, then another. Eventually when the swing returns to base, their centre, they're far happier.

The Bowl

This is seen when all the planets lie to one side of the zodiac, dividing the circle in half. The Bowl contains and holds the energies. It is opposed by an empty 6 houses so can find certain difficulties in life, with the empty houses. A sort of 'us' and 'them' scenario. Because of the intensity of the cluster in a Bowl shape I have found that clients are that: Intense. They also can find it more difficult to 'see' the other person's point of view. On the plus side they can powerfully focus on a task until it is complete.

Not good at multi-tasking!

The Bucket

The shape of this chart is where all the planets are on one side and one planet is opposite the others, representing the 'handle' of the Bucket.

On the plus side, this type dips deeply into life, is a real instructor and inspirer of others, and on the downside becomes an agitator and discontented person. Depending on where the singleton planet is located, is where the energies are strictly focused.

Again, like the Bowl there is intensity and it helps to understand the story and the energy of the lone singleton planet.

Make Your Chart

So go to www.astro.com and make up your chart and have a good look at it. Please don't use other websites! I'll tell you why. None of them will give you the option to choose the Equal House System. Go back to page 16 for the bits to click.

They're all programmed to use the Placidus house system, which unfortunately just doesn't give the same 'look' to a chart. It makes it look un-even and messy. Equal House makes at least one part of the chart look ordered, and that's the house sizes.
In Placidus the houses are all different sizes and for a beginner it makes things even more confusing.
Note your Ascendant which is displayed as ASC:
What Element is it: Earth, Air, Fire or Water?
What shape is your chart, is it a splash, a splay a bucket or a bowl or a see-saw?
Can you get a feel of your chart? Does it feel right for you?
If you don't know your birth time, don't panic, you can still make a chart.

I use a default time of 6am. You won't be creating an accurate chart but you can still get an idea of the signs of your planets and your chart shape.

Another helpful house system to use if you don't know your birth time is the one made popular by Robert Hand called Whole Sign. You could use this system for more ideas of your chart shape and the signs all your planets are in.
http://www.arhatmedia.com/whole_sign.html

However, this system is more suited to people that know about Astrology already. If you're a newbie stick with Equal House. And if you don't know your birth time you won't know the sign of your Ascendant or the order of your houses.

Starting to Understand Charts
So let's get out some charts and do a bit of Astrology. On the next page we have Elizabeth Barrett Browning's chart.

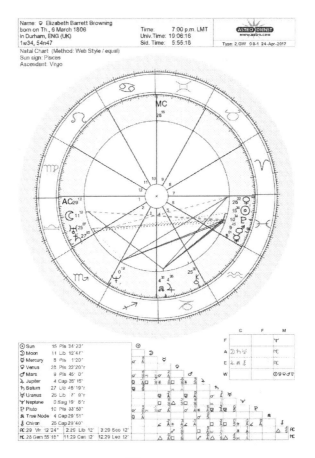

Figure 1

At first glance we can see all her planets are below the horizon because she was born late in the day. The Sun has gone down and wouldn't have been visible from earth at her time of birth.

With all her planets only on one side her chart shape therefore is a Bowl. This means she was a person more likely to focus on one task at a time and not quite so capable of 'seeing the bigger picture'.

However, that focus allowed her to follow her bliss, become a well-known and well-regarded poet AND to marry and live with the man she had strong feelings for. Even though it meant she had to lose the affection of her father in the process.

She was a Sun sign Pisces, with Moon in Libra and she had a Virgo Ascendant.
If we were to put her main astrological attributes into shorthand, this is what they'd say:
Likes attention to detail, concerned about her health (Virgo).
Romantic, unpractical and other-worldly (Pisces).
Interested in love/loving/relationship/s, wants things to be 'fair' (Libra).
Her Moon is also in the first house, near the Ascendant, and is the first planet in her chart, so her emotions are very near to 'the surface'.
Her chart shape is also very interesting as it's all one-sided. Bit like an Indigo's chart.
Using the Equal House System, (which I hope you are using too!) she has little clusters of planets in certain houses.
Three in the 1st and five in the 6th.
The first house is all about 'the self' and the 6th is all about health. She obviously was concerned about health issues, as not only did she have a Virgo Ascendant but Venus, Sun, Pluto, Mars and Mercury all in the 6th.
If we take into account some aspects, she has Sun conjunct Mercury (lots of people do) and also conjunct Pluto and Mars. Not quite as fluffy, as Pluto is all about obsession/transformation and Mars is the God of War.
The Virgo Ascendant also helps with writing ability.

She wrote a large number of poems and prose. Her first was self-published and printed by her father when she was 14[3] and she continued to write until her death aged 55.
During her courtship with her future husband Robert, between them they wrote 574 letters in 9 months. That's a LOT of writing!

Now don't worry too much if all of this seems complex, things will soon fall into place when you carry on making charts. Don't be scared or shy. Go to www.astro.com and make your chart. You don't have to do any calculations. It's all done for you!
What you will need to learn is the language that Astrologers use. All Astrological charts use symbols to represent the signs. It can be a bit tedious to start with to learn them, but the more charts you make, the quicker you'll learn what each symbol is.

Planet Symbols
What we'll start with is the symbols for some of the planets.

This is the symbol for the Sun. It's a circle with a dot in the centre. The dot represents individuality, with the circle surrounding it representing eternity.

The Moon symbol is pretty easy to recognise and is always written as a half Moon.

Mercury looks like the Venus symbol with a little half circle on its head. It is also known as the Winged Messenger God.

The Venus symbol is an international symbol representing the feminine. The circle of infinity, with the cross of the material world.

 Mars is another easily recognised symbol as it's one often used to represent the male.

It has the circle of infinity with the spear of War.

Sign Symbols

Now we'll do the signs, with their symbol meanings:

Symbol	Sign	Key Words
♈	Aries: Ram's Horns	Let me do it
♉	Taurus: Bull's Horns	Satisfy me
♊	Gemini: The Twins	Listen to me

Symbol	Sign	Key Words
♋	Cancer: The Breasts	Hug me
♌	Leo: Lion's Mane	Praise me
♍	Virgo: Female Virgin	Purify me
♎	Libra: Scales of Justice	Love me
♏	Scorpio: Scorpion's Sting	Trust me

Note: *The symbols for the Zodiac were devised before writing text was used. Virgo and Scorpio represent the female and male form.*

Symbol	Sign	Keywords
	Sagittarius: Archer's Arrow	Explore with me
	Capricorn: Goat with Fishy Tail	Respect me
	Aquarius: The Water Bearer	Liberate me
	Pisces: Two Fishes	Intuit me

OK, now you've got an overview of chart shapes, what each sign means, the symbols for each of them and the symbols for some of the planets and what they mean, you're well on the way to doing Astrology!

Well done!

Now we're going to cover a little more about the important planets we need to take into account when you're thinking about your love life and/or you are dating someone.

Chapter Two

How Do You Love?
Let Astrology Guide You

To truly understand your love life it helps to have a good understanding of your own birth chart and the romantic potential within it. We've already learned about the Ascendant and the Sun and Moon signs and chart shapes. Now we're going to learn about the planets that give us a deeper insight into how we love.

The planets we want to get a deeper understanding of are the love planets: Venus and Mars.

Venus is the Goddess of Love in Astrology and represents how we love and the sign it is in reveals in what way we receive love.

Mars is the God of War and represents our active energy and how we express it in a close personal relationship.

Mars Gives and Venus Receives

The Astronomy of Venus the Hot Planet
Venus is bright enough to be seen from the Earth with the naked eye. Like the Moon, it goes through phase changes, appearing as a bright light illuminated by the Sun, to a larger crescent, as it gets nearer to us, with some of it in shadow. Its surface is over twice as hot as your kitchen oven at 462 degrees centigrade day and night. It is the closest planet to the Earth and similar in size.

Like the Earth, Venus is also made of rock but its climate has 'gone out of control'.[4]
It is surrounded by a dense layer of clouds and underneath these clouds the Russian probe 'Venera 7', which landed on the surface in 1970, discovered the extreme heat temperatures on the planet's surface.

Other missions and probes sent back information but it wasn't until 1990 that a US spacecraft called 'Magellan' orbited with cloud-penetrating radars and found out that the surface is totally dry with evidence of volcanic eruptions.
Every now and then Venus' orbit means it crosses over the Sun. Sort of like a mini-eclipse. It can't block out the Sun like the Moon can, as it's further away from us. It makes a sort of black mark over its surface, which I don't recommend looking at, as that's dangerous to your eyes, you do need to use special lenses. The last eclipse was in June 2012 and will happen again in 2117, which is a bit of a long wait!

Venus in Astrology

Plenty has been written about the Astrology of Venus. Whole books. Articles. Websites. Most people agree that, like the Moon, Venus is a feminine planet in that to us on Earth, it looks as if it 'gives birth' to the day as it's only visible just as the day begins and also when it ends at sunset. And since humans invented Astrology, they thought it was a good idea to have masculine planets as well as feminine. Nice to know that ancient Astrologers were into equality within the sexes!

Of the 10 planets, the female ones are:
The Moon, Venus and Neptune.
The male ones are:
The Sun, Mars, Jupiter, Saturn and Pluto.

The unisex planets are:
Mercury and Uranus.

Venus is named after the Goddess of Love and Beauty. If you want an idea of what she represents, think of that wonderful painting *The Birth of Venus* by the Renaissance Italian painter Sandro Botticelli. She represents beauty, taste, love, art, luxury, harmony and pleasure. I say taste because I mean the sort of things you'd choose to decorate your home with or to wear. If your Venus is in disharmony with your partner's, you'll find he/she likes different colours or styles to you and you might argue about how you make your home look! She also represents money as without it you wouldn't be able to buy those things you desire and again, how/where Venus is placed in your chart will give you an idea of how you relate to your finances.

I won't repeat Venus' meanings for each of the twelve signs because plenty of other astrologers have already done that and you can read more about it on www.astro.com for yourself. What I will be pointing out is some short keywords and the relationship between each planet in your chart.

The Astronomy of Mars

The surface of Mars is covered with a layer of iron oxide or rust, which makes it look red from our view on earth. It is often called the red planet and most resembles Earth even though it is a lot smaller at just 4,222 miles in diameter. Unlike the Moon, Mars' surface is weathered by winds and its desert surface has seasonal dust storms. Various probes have been sent to the surface over the years and have discovered channels and gulleys, which appear to have been sculpted by running water.

Like the Earth, Mars has seasons and weather and it takes just over 24 hours to rotate once on its axis. However, it takes 687 days to orbit the Sun, which is far longer than our year of 365 days.[5]

During a winter on Mars, a third of its atmosphere can remain frozen above the polar ice caps. It also bears the scars of a heavy bombardment of meteoroids that formed impact craters and basins.

The USA's Mariner 4 first viewed it in 1965.

Then between 1971 and 1972 Mariner 9 viewed the planet.

In 1976 the US spacecraft Viking descended to its surface but produced inconclusive results.

During the 1990s the Mars Pathfinder landed in the Valley of Ares, which is rather fitting as a name! Since then further information has been recorded about its atmosphere, rock surface and weather conditions. In 1999 NASA's probe crash-landed. Then in October 2016 another probe called 'Schiaparelli', which was part of the European Space Agency's ExoMars programme – a joint venture with the Russians – also crash-landed. I can't say I'm upset about this, as my view is that we should leave these poor planets alone.

Mars is also host to two moons named Phobos and Deimos, named after two of Ares' sons according to Greek mythology.

The best time to observe Mars is when it is in opposition to (opposite) the Sun and closest to Earth. During this alignment of Mars, the Earth and the Sun, which takes place every 26 months, Mars' red glow can be seen with the naked eye. [6]

Mars in Astrology

Mars is the red planet, the colour of blood and emotion, and not surprisingly perhaps, God of War to the ancients. If Venus is the archetypal girlie of the solar system, Mars is the original lad, standing for ambition, competitiveness, willpower and the active pursuit of the attractive.

Mars was also the Roman God of War, and the planet Mars symbolises our aggressive nature. The appearance of the planet Mars with its fiery red colour, suggests action. We also tend to hear it being referred to as 'the angry red planet' and other such terms.

Mars represents how we go about getting the things we want, how we assert ourselves and express our independence and also how we defend ourselves when we are under attack. Mars is the complement to Venus, and both have to do with the mechanics of desire and attraction.

Words that are related to Mars are the name of the month March, the name of the planet Mars (hence the Martians), martial law and martial arts.

As Mars is the God of War he represents the *active* energy you put into your love life.

So, we can understand Venus represents how we *receive* love and Mars how we *give* it.

I've got both my Venus and Mars in the Air sign of Aquarius, so this was very confusing for me when I was a youngster as I'm a Water sign. There was me falling in love all the time with weird and different chaps and a lot of the time it all ended rather badly. When I began to recognise that my 'love planets' needed a bit of space and freedom it helped me to understand my love needs far more.

Sign Keywords

So, rather than give you lots of text about what-each-planet-means-in-each-sign, I'm just going to give you some keywords, so you can quickly get up to speed with what your love planets truly desire.

So, these are the keywords for each sign:

Aries: Let me do it
Taurus: Satisfy me
Gemini: Listen to me
Cancer: Hug me
Leo: Praise me
Virgo: Purify me
Libra: Love me
Scorpio: Trust me
Sagittarius: Explore with me
Capricorn: Respect me
Aquarius: Liberate me
Pisces: Intuit me

Now, find out the sign of your Venus and Mars and write a sentence using the words above.

Let's use our chart example.

Elizabeth had Venus and Mars in Pisces.
So if we were to write a sentence about how she'd liked to give and receive love it would be:

I like to receive love in an intuitive way and to give it in an intuitive way.
I want to use my intuition in my love life.

In Robert's chart, he's got his Venus in Cancer and his Mars in Gemini.

Bit more tricky to satisfy him!

I like to receive lots of hugs and to give my love by writing or talking about it.
I want to use hugs and be listened to in my love life.

As you can see, between their various planets, there's a lot going on.

Robert's Venus gets along nicely with Elizabeth's Venus and Mars because they're all in water signs, but his Mars is in Air and needs that extra amount of chat/discussion/conversation to feel 'heard'.

Yoko has Venus in Aquarius and Mars in Virgo
Here is how we could express her love needs:

I like to receive love in a liberating way and to give my love in a pure way.
I want to use liberation and purity in my love life

John has Venus in Virgo and Mars in Libra and his love needs could be expressed this way:

I like to receive love in a pure way and to give my love in a loving way
I want to use purity and love in my love life

John and Yoko had a nice little combo with Virgo in their love-life as they had what's called a Venus and Mars conjunction (this gets Astrologers quite excited) as it means their two love-planets were actually talking with each other because they're in the *same sign.*

In the other direction, both Yoko's Venus and John's Mars were in Air signs, which is the element that likes LOTS of discussion.

In my series of Sun sign books for each sign, I also used these keywords, which are similar to the previous list:

Aries: Appreciate
Taurus: Satisfy
Gemini: Listen to
Cancer: Care for
Leo: Lavish
Virgo: Soothe
Libra: Love
Scorpio: Win the Trust of
Sagittarius: Believe in
Capricorn: Cheer Up
Aquarius: Bond
Pisces: Survive

You can mix and match the words. We're just getting a feel of your chart and what your love needs are. You might find that the planets in your chart are all in different signs.
What then?
Maybe you're a more complex character and need different inputs to feel centred.
There's no right or wrong.
Getting to know your planets takes time, so don't rush things. You're doing great. Keep learning.
Now nothing in life is perfect, so don't get downhearted if your love planets and your intended's planets don't seem to resonate so well.

Always, always remember to take the whole chart into account, not just teeny bits of it. And as I will keep repeating, it doesn't matter what happens in your respective charts, if you're not actually having a relationship, then Astrology won't make it happen!!

Now that you've found out about Venus and Mars we are going to go a little deeper into your love life.

Chapter Three

What Are You Really Looking For in a Relationship?

Something I always suggest to people who are looking for a partner, is to be clear about what it is that you want.

To be *absolutely* clear: what you want, not what you *don't* want.

Plenty of people who have been in bad relationships will give me endless examples of what they *don't* want.
They *don't* want someone who ignores them or is nasty to them or worse.
They *don't* want someone married, or with baggage.
They *don't* want local people or foreign people or people of a different religion or thought process.
It gets worse.
When people are in a sad, resentful-filled place they say things like:
'All men are bastards.' (There is even an Astrology book with that in the title, how unhelpful is that!)

'All women just want one thing: money, children.'

STOP!

PLEASE stop telling the Universe about the things you *don't* want.

Tell The Universe What You Want

Start telling the Universe what you *do* want.

Have a look at the feed on your social media account or listen to your friends that are single, and the one who's been single the longest will write/say things like:

'I'm 37. I'm single-ish. Lived by myself for 18 years and have no intention of changing that. I don't do marriage or mortgages. Again it doesn't really interest me. This doesn't make me different in a bad way nor does it make me weird or have some kind of issues. Neither am I heart broken blah blah blah. So please stop judging.'

or

'All my men crushes are actually such bastards.'

or

'Men are all the same - lying, cheating bastards.'

or

'Are all men selfish, pig headed bastards or is it just the ones I know?'

or

'All women are "crazy" you just have to find the crazy one that you can handle.'

or

'I realised all women are crazy when I realised how crazy my mum is lol.'

Now, if you think that every message or post or thing you say is a reflection of something *within* you, writing or saying anything like this will be an expression of your inner deeper self. And what's *in* your inner self will keep being given to you unless you make a few personal tweaks and changes. Also if you keep moaning that all men/women are bastards/only-after-one-thing, then that's what you're telling the Universe (or your deeper, inner self) and all the Universe will give back to you.

The Universe doesn't know the difference between what you want and what you don't want. All it will 'hear' is what you're talking about, so be very careful what you say. What we give out will become what we get, so be very careful about what you give out into the world.

So have a think about what it is you're saying/doing that might be attracting these 'bad' relationships.

Sometimes it's due to lack of self-confidence.

Sometimes it's because you might never have had a nice relationship with someone, so you're not sure what one would be like. This book will help you have a better understanding of what fun a less challenging relationship can be like.

Make A List

Just like going food shopping in a supermarket without making a list causes you to get things you didn't go in for, the same happens when you're searching for a partner.

MAKE A LIST!

It doesn't have to be anything out of this world, or complex. Just the basic qualities you'd like your Perfect, or at least, Nearly-Perfect Partner to have.
I
f you want to have children with them, write that on your list.

If you don't want to actually give birth, put that too.

If you want to get married in a church with all the trimmings, make sure you write that down.

If you'd prefer your ideal partner to be single, working... whatever, write that down.

I'm amazed how many people tell me they want to meet Mr or Miss Right but they have no idea of the qualities or practical considerations of the person they'd like to meet.

Now, you can't use Astrology to *find* your ideal partner, but you can use it to find when you're more likely to *meet* that person.

Most people have had at least one relationship by the time they reach their Saturn return at approx age 28-30. You're also more likely to be love-successful during a Venus or Mars transit, which we will cover in Chapter Five.

Ask and You Shall Receive

To get a good idea of what you're really looking for in a relationship, start thinking about what you truly want.

Be realistic.

If you don't hang about with very rich people, the chances of you meeting someone who is a millionaire are very, very slim.

The sorts of things that are good to ask for are:

Someone who understands you.

Someone who enjoys your company and/or going out and/or enjoys quiet time too.

Someone you can love *and* like.

Maybe add a few things about what you'll do together, such as trips to the beach/festivals/concerts.

If you like travelling, then add that.

The best things to ask for are personal qualities such as:

Trustfulness, peaceful outlook, kindness, friendliness, helpfulness, forgivingness, cheerfulness, patience, gratitude, courtesy, faithfulness, warmth, consideration and fairness.

A lot of people write 'good sense of humour' but humour is very personal, so if you're asking about the humour thing, make sure you add that they have a *similar* sense of humour to you. If you're sarcastic or ironic and enjoy that, put it in.

There are no judgements here. I can't tell you what to ask for. I can only make suggestions.

Marriage or Not

If you want to be married, please write that in your letter. If you don't, make it very clear about what sort of relationship you want to have.

Do you want to be partners?

Lovers?

Friends?

Do you want to live together?

Or apart?

And if you don't want to marry, do you want to have some sort of celebration like a hand-fasting? Or troth pledging? Or broom-jumping?

And if you don't want to marry, why not?

Have you thought further into the future about what *not* being married means where you live, in your culture?

Some of my clients in the UK have the mistaken belief that living together makes them 'common-law' and that they have as many rights as married people. This is not true.

Common-law spouses

Although the terms common-law wife or husband are frequently used to describe a couple who live together, these relationships do not have legal recognition.[7] If one or other of you dies, you have no legal claim on anything belonging or relating to that person unless you made a legally binding arrangement with a solicitor beforehand.

Civil Partnerships

A civil partnership is a legal relationship which can be registered by two people of the same sex who aren't related to each other. If you are in a same-sex relationship, registering a civil partnership will give your relationship legal recognition. This will give you added legal rights, as well as responsibilities.

In the US it's the same.

The Myth

There is a common misperception that if you live together for a certain length of time you are common-law married. This is not true anywhere in the U.K or United States.[8]

Platonic Relationships

A platonic relationship is one 'confined to words or theory, not leading to action, purely spiritual, not sexual.'
In the work I do, I don't come across them much. Well, not ones where the clients themselves call the relationship they have platonic but I do think they need to be discussed. A regular relationship could become purely platonic if either or both partner develops an illness or disability that prevents sexual expression.
I have had clients that have never had a sexual relationship. Family problems, abuse, religion, or physical issues have prevented them having a relationship with anyone.
They have close friendships but that's where relationships stop.

One gentleman I worked with was in his 60s. He was an Aquarius, one of the only signs who can live more easily 'in their heads' than in their bodies. He had a nice life, didn't have to work, had enough money, was very interested in Astrology and was happy with his life. He had friends though and I know if he didn't have any friends, he would have been bereft.

For a platonic relationship to truly work, both partners must agree on the terms of their relationship. Talking about it helps. Keeping quiet and hoping your partner will understand doesn't.

I think we need to make the distinction that a love relationship is one where that love is expressed in more ways than one: mental, emotional, physical (and if you're very lucky) spiritual.

A platonic relationship is still a relationship but it doesn't involve physical expression. And there also needs to be a distinction between a friendship and a platonic relationship. A friendship does not involve sex. If it does, it's a regular relationship.

Some people have non-physical relationships that are only on-line. They worry about, think about, talk about their 'partner'... but never actually meet in the flesh. They can continue for years.

Divorce

I'm told time and time again by people that have been divorced: *'I never want to marry ever again!'*

I've discovered that this sentence isn't actually a true statement, because what lies underneath that statement is the reality that they don't want to re-marry the person they have just divorced. Most of the time, after divorce, if you meet 'The One' you will naturally want to formalise the relationship in some way.

So please don't write in your letter to the Universe, that you don't want to re-marry.

Ask for someone who will have the same view as you about marriage, because you can guarantee if you tell the Universe *'I never want to marry again'* you'll be chased by potential partners who want to do just that: Get Married.

So be very clear about what you want, not what you don't want.

Any requesting of the Universe must be written in the positive, not the negative.

I made the following mistake in my request to the Universe, having been married then divorced. In my letter I accidently wrote *'I want to meet someone who has experienced marriage.'*

I wanted to meet someone who understood what marriage was all about. Who knew about domestic things like food shopping and paying bills and taking in turns to do things. Who understood what marriage is.

When what I really meant was: *'I want to meet someone who has experienced marriage and is now divorced'*.

Unfortunately when I met The One he was legally married (but separated) so I had to endure his divorce. So be very careful about what you write! The Universe will always give you what you ask for!

Children

Just as you might want to think about how or if to marry, you might want to also give some thought to children. Do you want to have any? Do you want to become a parent? And if you're a parent already and looking for love, do you want more children with your new partner?

Having children can make or break a relationship, as it's a life-changing decision and one you can't back out of once the child/ren is/are born. It's also great fun. I loved being a parent (I still do). It's a totally different form of love than that which you share with a partner and our relationship is fab, so my experience is positive. But some people have such dreadful childhoods they vow never to have children themselves and inflict those negative energies onto another generation.

If you truly want to have children, then please do not date someone who has clearly stated they don't want children. They're not going to change their minds just because you're hoping they will and also wanting something different to your partner means you've got non-aligned life outlooks, and that's hard to live with. I do know people who have had kids 'by mistake' in the hope that the chap will stay with them. It never works. Please don't do it!

So, if you really don't want children, then please use contraceptives. There is no way you can just hope for the best. Be practical. And this advice applies to men as much as women. If you don't want to become a Dad at all, or yet, then it's even more your responsibility to use a contraceptive.
At the other end of the scale, there are people who, for whatever reason, can't have children but want them.

There isn't space in this little book to cover that subject Astrologically, but there are ways and means of determining if your predicament is permanent or capable of healing.

OK, so now you're completely clear about what you want in a relationship. Let's go a little further with Astrology.

You might have noticed already that the birth chart is divided into 12 segments.
Well spotted!!
These are called houses.

If you don't know your birth time, you'll have to ignore the subject of houses as it can only be calculated with an accurate birth time.

Astrological Houses

If you look at a birth chart, you will see that there are 12 segments to it. Bit like slices of pizza. Each one of those segments is called a 'house' because it is the home of your planets in your personal chart. And where something is located is important to its expression.

Location, Location, Location

We used to have an enormously tall tree next to our house.

Lovely tree and had probably stood there for more than 30 years. But as lovely as it was, it blocked the light into the house and was so tall eventually I was worried its roots would get under that side of our house.

Great tree.

Challenging location.

If it had been planted in a big expansive garden or park, it would have stood tall and strong and been fine. But in our teeny suburban back garden, it was now out of place. It's a similar thing in Astrology. Where a planet is located in your chart is either easy, or challenging, and if it's challenging there are always solutions.

The houses are numbered 1-12 and go anti-clockwise round the chart.

Each house has a different meaning.

Here is a quick rundown of each house's meaning:

The First House: Personality
The Second House: Money, Material Possessions and Self-Worth
The Third House: Communication & Short Journeys
The Fourth House: Home, Family & Roots
The Fifth House: Creativity & Romance

The Sixth House: Work & Health
The Seventh House: Relationships & Marriage
The Eighth House: Life Force in Birth, Sex, Death &
After-Life
The Ninth House: Philosophy & Long Distance Travel
The Tenth House: Social Identity & Career
The Eleventh House: Social Life & Friendships
The Twelfth House: Spirituality, Secrets and The
Hidden Self

The two houses we are going to concentrate on as far
as love, romance and marriage go are the **Fifth** and
Seventh houses.
Now, because everyone is different, we will all have
different signs for each house.
My fifth house might be in the sign of Capricorn and
yours might be in Scorpio. The different *signs* of your
houses are because your chart *starts* in a different
sign.

The Fifth House

The fifth house is the segment of your chart that lets
us know a little about your attitude to romance and
creativity. If your Sun is placed here, you'll seriously
enjoy the whole caboodle of love and loving and
smoochie-ness. You'll want to be followed by men
bearing gifts of flowers and chocolates and if you're a
bloke, you'll enjoy romantic evenings with
candlelight, beautiful music et al.

As there are 10 planets that we use in Astrology, any
one of them could easily end up in this house... or
not. I've got my Saturn and Jupiter located here,
which is a bit tricky as they're two totally different
planets.
Whatever planet/s you do have here, will have an
influence on how you gel with romance.

For ladies it also gives a sneak peak at fertility, as this is the house that represents the ultimate creation of our children.

Please don't fret if you don't have any planets here, every few days the Moon will transit through it, bringing its blessings.

Here's a very brief list of what it could mean to have the following planets in this house:
Sun - You want to shine in the area of love and romance.
Moon - You have an emotional attitude to love and romance.
Mercury - You want to talk about love and romance.
Venus - You want love to be fair and beautiful.
Mars - You feel energised and active when you're in love.
Jupiter - What are your beliefs about Love?
Saturn - How serious do you want love to be?
Uranus - You need plenty of freedom to love, or not.
Neptune - Are you 'in love' with love?
Pluto - Power and transformation go deeply in your love-life.

The Seventh House

This is traditionally the marriage house, so can contain interesting information or suggestions about the sort of person you may ultimately settle down with. I've got my Sun sign in Pisces located here, so even though I got divorced, I was on a mission to find The One and get re-married.

When I read for single clients that have Sun in the 7th, I always know they'll feel heaps better when they are united with the one they can love.

Here are some further meanings for the various planets you could have in your marriage house.

Sun - Your Life Purpose is to be in a relationship.
Moon - Your feelings guide you in partnerships.
Mercury - You want to be able to talk with your partner.
Venus - You want your relationship to be fair and beautiful.
Mars - You feel energised and active when you're with the one you love.
Jupiter - You want your partner to believe in you.
Saturn - You take a serious attitude to relationships.
Uranus - You need plenty of freedom in any relationship.
Neptune - You have an idealised/spiritual/fantasy approach to relationships.
Pluto - You want your relationship to deeply change you.

The Descendant

Using Astrology we can tell quite a bit about what we are looking for in a relationship by checking the 7th house, or the descendant sign.

We've covered the Ascendant in Chapter One. The Descendant is directly opposite the Ascendant and will be in the opposite sign.

So the sign of your Descendant will explain what you're actually looking for in a close, personal relationship, which will be completely opposite to how you project yourself.

The Ascendant starts at the 1st house.
The Descendant is located at the 7th house.

Back to our chart example.

Elizabeth has a Virgo Ascendant and the opposite sign to Virgo is Pisces.

So her 7th house starts in the sign of Pisces.

As we're using Equal House most of her 7th house is in the sign of Aries, which is the sign of the leader, so in a way, she wanted to lead the relationship.

Which she did as when Robert made suggestions, sometimes forcibly (as he had Moon in Aries), she either conceded or didn't. It took him more than a year to persuade her to leave her family and marry him and he did it by reassuring her constantly. All that Virgo-ness wanted attention to detail, perfection and for all the small things to be in place before she could even contemplate the Big Move.

And on the plus point, as Robert had Moon in Aries, his Moon affected Elizabeth's 7th house as they're both in the same sign.

More on this in Chapter Six.

Remember the keywords from before about how each sign expresses itself:
Aries: Let me do it
Taurus: Satisfy me
Gemini: Listen to me
Cancer: Hug me
Leo: Praise me
Virgo: Purify me
Libra: Love me
Scorpio: Trust me
Sagittarius: Explore with me
Capricorn: Respect me
Aquarius: Liberate me
Pisces: Intuit me

Sun and/or Moon in the Seventh

What sign is your 7th house in? Is your 7th house in a sign that *wants* a partner? Or does it work better on its own?
Are there any planets in your 7th house?
The two planets that are more likely to want a relationship, no matter what, are the Sun or Moon in the 7th.
People with a Libra Ascendant, or Sun in the 7th (which Astrologically are nearly the same thing) will not feel right in themselves when they're single.
People with a Leo Ascendant or Sun in the 5th, will really like the whole romance thing. They'll love the courting phase of dating, and will yearn for that romance and want to re-ignite it regularly.

If you've got Moon in the 7th or 5th the issues above will still apply but you'll be far more emotional about the whole thing, so make sure you look after those emotions.

Now, as there are zillions of different combinations you can have with the 7th and 5th, I can't give all of those to you. But do the work yourself. Make it easy. Just put the above words into your 7th and see how that feels for you.
Does it feel right?

Don't worry if yours are empty.

Every month the Moon will transit through those houses, giving you a little boost of relationship energy.

Equally, twice a year for about a month, the Sun, Venus and Mars will transit through those houses, again giving you a positive relationship boost. And at other stages in your life the other planets might also make their way through this part of your chart. We'll discuss this in more detail in Chapter 5

Chapter Four

The Relationship You Have Versus The One You Could Have

Up until now we've been talking about finding 'The One'. In this chapter I'm going to talk about the relationship you might be in already.

Some relationships stand out as truly loving and I'm going to use the charts of two sets of people who there is no dispute, truly loved each other.
I searched for quite a while to find some Fire sign relationships that have lasted (famous ones that is) or Gemini ones, and they don't exist!
Anyway, I will also cover what happens when a Fire sign gets together with a Water sign and how it can all go horribly wrong...
Now, please don't misunderstand me, there are plenty of people that are supposedly 'incompatible' but manage to make very lasting relationships.
I haven't used an Aries example, as you can't advise an Aries in relationships. Once they decide someone is going to be their partner, the more you question or protest, the harder they will dig their heels in and proclaim undying love!
David Beckham (Taurus) is, at the time of writing, married to Victoria (Aries) and their relationship is apparently happy. They have children and everyone seems content. Victoria does have a Cancer Ascendant, so that's obviously the saving grace for their partnership. She's loyal to him, he to her, what more do you want?

However, please don't get fooled by the Ascendant sign.

The Ascendant will carry your relationships for quite a while. It will allow you to fall deeply in love... but it's not going to satisfy your love relationships for too long if you ignore the actual Sun sign you're with.

First Impressions

My first marriage seemed successful. I have Leo Ascendant and my ex has Sagittarius.

Both Fire signs and compatible.

I have Moon in Gemini and my ex is Sun Gemini.

All Hunky Dory.

Except my ex has Moon in Taurus, (like my first love) and that really doesn't gel with my Gemini Moon.

Not only should the Sun signs get on, but compatible Moons make for *emotional* comfort too.

If you only look at the Ascendant sign, you can very easily be deceived. It all seems lovely at the beginning... you trust each other, nothing can go wrong, the world is at your feet... everything seems comfortable and do-able.

When the dust settles there has to be more than just that Ascending sign holding your relationship together.

If your Suns and Moons aren't talking, then it will seem, after a while, that you're not being heard or understood by your partner, which is a horrible feeling.

My second husband has a Libra Ascendant and that works nicely with my Leo Ascendant
He also has Moon in Sagittarius, which is opposite my Moon and means we understand each other's feelings well. His Moon is Fire and mine is Air, so they work much better together.

When I read about instant romances, with a marriage happening minutes later, I always wonder if it's the Ascendants that are the attraction, not the Sun signs. A compatible Ascendant is a very strong draw. You can very easily get sucked into its wonderfulness but I would argue that making a note of it and working with what's *underneath* might prevent you from heartache and upsetment later. Forewarned is forearmed...

Chart Examples

The two sets of examples I am using to demonstrate astrological compatibility and deep love are the poets Elizabeth Barrett Browning and her husband Robert Browning, and John Lennon and his wife Yoko Ono. Elizabeth was a Pisces with Moon in Libra.
Robert was a Taurus with Moon in Aries.
See pages 22 and 94.

John was Sun in Libra and Yoko is an Aquarius. Both their birth times are A-rated, so are as accurate as possible. See page 97.

We don't have a totally accurate birth time for Robert but if the info I found is correct, his Ascendant was possibly Sagittarius. However, we definitely do have accurate data for Elizabeth and for both of them we do have accurate birth dates.

As I mentioned earlier, poets have a way with words.

Now, whether or not Elizabeth and Robert were as blissfully happy in their relationship as their poetry suggests, we just don't know. What we do know is they stayed together for at least 15 happy years until Elizabeth sadly died after the multiple deaths of her father, a good friend and her sister when she was 55 years old. Elizabeth and Robert had one child, a son, who was also a Pisces with his Moon in Virgo, just like his mother. He never had children, so their family line ended with him.

Robert got very excited when he met Elizabeth and his poetry reflects his falling deeply in love. Here's one I like:

My Star

ALL that I know
    Of a certain star
Is, it can throw
    (Like the angled spar)
Now a dart of red,
    Now a dart of blue;
Till my friends have said
    They would fain see, too
My star that dartles the red and the blue!
Then it stops like a bird; like a flower, hands furled:
    They must solace themselves with the Saturn above it.
What matter to me if their star is a world?
    Mine has opened its soul to me; therefore I love it.[9]

More about our lovers later. Let's concentrate on what your experiences might be...

Your Relationship

So what sort of relationship do you have?
What is it about it that you're struggling with?

Projection

What I like about Astrology, is it prevents projection.
Projection is a term used in psychology to describe
accusing someone else of having qualities you've not
recognised in yourself. A woman might say that her
husband is jealous all the time, when she's the one
with the jealousy problem. She only sees in others the
flaws she can't recognise in herself.

Astrology allows us to step back from ourselves and
'see' our place in our world and how we are. Which is
why learning about your own chart is FAR more
important than learning about your partner's. When
your relationship is already formed, THEN you can
explore what your partner needs and how to fulfil
those needs.

Complex Relationships

I don't know if relationships are any more complex
than they might have been in the past. Who knows? It
doesn't really matter if they were or were not. What
does matter, and makes a relationship much more
difficult, is the opinion of 'others'.

When you start to date, getting the opinion of your
friends seems important BUT it will only cloud and
confuse things. On the one hand you want a
relationship and on the other you don't want to lose
those friendships from school or work or college.

Here is Victoria talking about an early relationship
she had in her teens. She's a Gemini and she had
strong feelings for a Scorpio lad called Alexander.

'Alexander was pretty, we liked the same music, we talked a lot (I met him over the internet, on a fanclub of a band)... And I thought I fell in love.'

However

'He never specifically asked me to be his girlfriend.'

This is a key point.

If Mr. Right doesn't ask you out, or ask to date, or take you on a date or make any sort of move, then he's not interested. PLEASE remember this!

Being a Gemini and an Air sign means conversation is very important. Feeling heard and understood is top of her wish list. However, right at the beginning of the relationship (for her) he said something she would have benefited by listening to:

'He called me and told me we should take a break in our relationship and concentrate on our schoolwork and exams, and if after that we still feel like being together, we will be.'
So, the poor lad was *trying* to break it to her gently that he's not interested in continuing the relationship/friendship but she ignores his advice as she's convinced there is more to discover.

'Our mutual friends would later tell me: "I saw you were in love with him, I was just waiting for you to admit it to yourself." I talked to his best friend (I had contacts with a few of his friends) and arranged that I would come to his town and she would arrange a meeting for us.'

They had a fling, a one-night stand so Victoria would have, as she said: *'Because I wanted a memory. And he was my first, so that is quite a memory.'*

I'm sure she wouldn't want to re-do her memories and maybe they've now helped her understand the difference between a simple, loving relationship and a stressful-angst-filled encounter.

This gentleman had a similar problem. He dated someone at University when they were both 19. Even though she reciprocated his affection, eventually life took over and they parted.

'The last time I saw her was for her Birthday in May 1980. We made love one last time, and her image from that time is with me still. I loved her then and I suppose a part of me will always love her.
She went on to write for The Guardian Newspaper in London, and has, I'm delighted to say, done well. As I suppose, all things considered, have I.'

If Only...
You might have the idea that if-only-my-mother-in-law-was-less-critical-I'd-be-happier or if-only-my-partner's-boss-was-nice-I'd-feel-more-content. Thinking like this relies on something that might never happen. Maybe your mother-in-law will never stop being critical, or your partner's boss will never be nicer. What then?
Relationships don't operate in a vacuum, and the people around you will all have some input on your relationship. Some of them will even have an investment in it! But to be truly happy we have to resist the temptation to allow those 'others' to affect our own personal feelings.

If you and your partner were marooned on a desert island, do you think your relationship would survive?

Or is your relationship dependent on your parents' input or your friends' or even your children's?

The complexity of your relationship is solely down to you, not the circumstances surrounding it. I know people who live challenging lives and their relationships are reasonably blissful and empowering.

Others crumble when one partner gets bored. I certainly don't advocate staying in a challenging relationship but is your relationship as challenging as you think? Or is the challenge within yourself?

Clients I counsel come for help for the following reasons:

Affairs

Having an affair is a big one. It's not always simple either. The affair might be with someone the same sex as the client and then involves 'coming out' as well as explaining their sexuality to their children. Aquarius and Sagittarius are the two signs most in need of freedom in a relationship and if one partner is too possessive, they'll run a mile. Gemini likes variety and can also very speedily get bored in a relationship if there isn't a lot of change.

Sometimes people have affairs because they're bored, or they're tempted by the excitement of doing something 'naughty', or their present partner's sexual appetite isn't the same as theirs. Or has wavered. Affairs start for a million different reasons but generally because somewhere in the history of the affair-risking person is some unresolved grief or anger.

Gambling and Addiction

This will destroy almost any relationship, even if both partners are indulging. If this is in your relationship, get some counselling. Ask for help. Investigate AA or other charities that will help. Again, underneath the addiction or the gambling behaviour will be some problem from the past that needs to heal. Take urgent steps towards recovery. True love can't exist in a toxic environment.

Fancying or Loving Someone Else

This is very much Gemini and Pisces territory. I once worked out that the majority of on-line serial daters were either Gemini or Pisces and the sign least likely to be on a dating site is Taurus, as they don't like change.

Mind you, loving someone other than the person you are with can happen to any sign, it's just that the mutable signs are more prone to want change and variety.

The actress Elizabeth Taylor: Pisces Sun, Moon Scorpio (who married her Scorpio husband twice) was a victim of serial marriages. Eight marriages in her lifetime. She died aged 79.

The Problems with In-Laws

This can cause an enormous amount of grief and discord in a relationship. When you become someone's partner or get married, their family, parents, siblings, uncles and aunts also have some investment in your relationship.

Depending on your upbringing and social and cultural expectations, the mother-in-law can either be a blessing or a curse.

It can help to check your own chart against your in-laws and find a place of similarity and work on that.

Also it won't help your peace of mind if you continually worry about what your in-laws might think about you. Stay focused only on what they actually say or do. Anything else is just unhelpful Mind Stuff.

I've worked with numerous clients who have awful in-laws. They don't like the way they 'tell' them how to bring up the children, or how to cook or what work they should or shouldn't be doing. After a time, this constant badgering can wear any sane human being down. Don't wait until you're desperate to get some help. The deep relaxation you can find from a good Hypnotherapy session can help you feel calmer and less aggravated. Being in a calmer state of mind will also help you make better decisions.

Also, try not to make your in-laws The Enemy.

Do your best to talk about them in more positive terms. Don't label them in your words or your mind, or you'll find your words will become a self-fulfilling prophecy.

Becoming Parents

Becoming a parent can put some marriages or relationships under a lot of strain. Most people manage the extra effort needed but for some the new person in their lives becomes an issue. If your relationship was wobbly before you have children, it won't miraculously get better after you give birth. If you're lucky, the Astrology of your child's chart will help you. There might be past-life connections or this-life compatibility. When you compare your charts, make sure you use both Mum and Dad's charts as sometimes one or other parent gets along better with the child and the chart will show the reason why.

Step-Children

Again this is an area with the potential for maximum upsetment. You might meet Mr or Ms Right and they have children and you are now a step-parent. Are you managing OK? Do you want to make things right but find it hard? My husband became a step-parent to my son when we married and he must have found it hard at times to not get involved in the parenting thing as my son said that since he already had a dad, he didn't want my husband to parent him. Which we all agreed on.

However one in six men in their 30s are stepfathers raising other men's children, nearly double the proportion of a decade ago. Stepfamilies are the fastest growing family type.[10]

Don't suffer in silence.

Read this fab book *How to be a Happy Stepmum* by Dr Lisa Doodson if you're a stepmum. I couldn't find a good book about being a stepdad but in the UK there is a good charity called Families Need Fathers.[12]

Most importantly, check out the Astrology of everyone involved. In the same way we will be looking at and understanding you and your partner's charts, do check out the charts of your stepchildren and find good points of commonality.

Disappointment

Now this is a biggie. There you are dating Mr or Ms Totally Right and three months down the line it all falls apart. Why is that?
Remember how I talked about when people are dating they're looking for someone like themselves? Well, think of it this way. Say you were to meet your double, would you get along well?
I've noticed this far too many times to ignore this little piece of wisdom:
If you have a bad relationship with your 'self' you'll have even *worse* relationships with other people.
There you are moaning that your partner does or doesn't do something that you love or hate, when the emphasis would be better spent on making your 'self' feel better.

This is where Astrology is our Saving Grace.
In less than the time it takes to make a pot of tea and have a snack, you can find out if your intended IS like you or if it's all an illusion you're suffering from.
The disappointment that people feel when they realise that Mr or Ms Totally Right isn't actually Totally Right is in proportion to how much you need to learn FAR more about your 'self'.

Now I am writing this on a nice sunny day with the winter sun streaming through the blinds and I'm making a rational case for what happens in relationships. You could very easily accuse me of not knowing at all how it feels for you to be in this bad space.

But, trust me, I've been there too.

As we know, relationships are as far away from rational thought as they can be. In fact probably even further. When you're in the throes of newly dating/learning about someone all rational thought can fly away so far, it's difficult to get your brain back where it used to be. Which is in your head. It's as if parts of your brain have wandered off into the desert and are now really, really thirsty and hungry and you'll do anything to stop the pain and agony.

Allow your 'self' some space.

Meeting Your Self

Allow your 'self' a bit of mental space to actually determine if what you're feeling is because you've met this wonderful person, or is because you've met your 'self'.

And do you actually like that 'self' that you've met? Sometimes when we're dating, the whole process can spark off learning something about our inner needs. It can be amazingly exciting. I've seen it happen. It's also happened to me. Everything is roses, flowers, sparkly lights and immense swings from good feelings to bad. It's very tiring and exhausting. Then one day you wake up and it all seems to have stopped. And you start to look for flaws in the person you were madly in love with yesterday.

Where before all you saw was the good, now you see only the bad, and that's not a nice discovery. The mind is a wonderful and equally terrible thing, especially when it's allowed to run free with no self awareness.

Finding out about your 'self' is far more empowering than coming face-to-face with yourself via a partner. Often all those things you love and hate about them, you love and hate about your 'self'.

The Magnificent Relationship

I worked with a client who fell madly, and deeply in love with someone who was already in a relationship. His feelings kicked in so quickly and so strongly he risked his job, his marriage and his sanity trying to get Ms Totally (in his mind) Right to notice him, to date him, to go out with him for a coffee or come out for a meal, or a drink or maybe something more. It went on for quite a while. Luckily his Higher Self finally kicked in and brought him a serious medical condition that he had to face and address.

His energies then were spent on his *own* health and needs, rather than chasing the dream of this magnificent relationship he'd conjured up in his mind.

Their Astrology was quite good. Both Air signs, both sharing good aspects. But Ms Totally Right was much older than him. And at the time that this happened, Uranus the planet of freedom was opposite his Sun sign, and Jupiter the planet of making-things-bigger-and-Belief was aspecting his Mercury.

So on the one hand he was fed-up being married with all the responsibilities that came with that (Uranus) and on the other his thoughts went into overdrive with thinking too much that she was the answer to all his dreams (Jupiter).

She wasn't the answer to all his dreams.

She was just a nice lady.

A very nice lady.

But she wasn't going to make his life any better, or more fun, or make him feel any different.
And anyway, she was already with someone!
He did go into a bit of a meltdown but came out the other side with a much clearer idea of who he is and how he wants to live his life.
So if you get to that place of disappointment, carefully study your chart.
Learn everything you can about what makes you happy or sad. What you enjoy and what you feel better avoiding.

Study your own Astrology, not Mr or Ms Right's.
Once you understand that you are truly different to anyone else on the planet (even if you're a twin) then you can appreciate more that your partner is different to you and might have different needs. Then you can fulfil those needs without compromising your own.

I've got Moon in Gemini, so I know full well that I get drastically bored doing the same thing day in day out and I love having lots of little things to do here and there and I love dividing my day into lots of little projects.
My lovely husband has Moon in Sagittarius (liking intellectual voyages) in the 3rd (enjoys lots of emotional, varied stimulus) so he feels better working on something creative or artistic (he's an artist now!) and when he has a new project on the go he's happy.
We both find it harder to focus on anything for a long time, so we're happier when we divide our time up with dog walks, short journeys and variety.

How to Make Things Better

OK.

Now we've discussed some of the things that can happen in a relationship. Let's do some Astrology so we can help you avoid all these potential problems. The best way to use Astrology to help you have a more successful relationship is to work out what it is/was that our chart examples have, that you could model that would improve the relationship you are in.

What was it about these people that made their relationships so loving and lasting?

And what action can you take to make things better?

Aspects

An aspect is an Astrological term for the degrees between planets and certain ones help relationships gel.

The Astrology that makes things *better* are aspects called conjunctions, trines and sextiles.

These are astrological relationships between planets in your chart that are friendlier and less stressful.

If you've got at least one of these in your chart, then you're on the road to making your love life much more empowering.

I haven't (as yet) come across someone who doesn't have at least one of these aspects in their chart and when you find yours FOCUS on it.

Give it all your attention. Nurture it, as it will allow you to work better and smarter with the more challenging aspects, which are the opposition, square and inconjunct.

Let the Website Take the Strain

At the bottom of most charts that www.astro.com produces, you'll see a grid with all the aspects in your chart. This gives you an idea of which planets are chatting with other planets in your chart. These are mathematical relationships and the computer programme luckily calculates this all for you. Back in the day you'd have to work all this out yourself. I'm SO glad I wasn't an Astrologer then! I'd get a headache will all the work needed!

Conjunction

A conjunction is Astro-speak for when two planets are very close together in the same sign or at least only a few degrees apart.

Astrologers are, as we've discussed, interested in the planets' placements in the sky from our view from earth, so the consideration is whether they're in the same *section* (or sign) of the sky... and that is called a conjunction.

Now, we discovered earlier that our Astrological Sky is divided into 12 segments, each one named after (what was) a constellation of stars... starting with Aries in the Spring Solstice time of the year... and a conjunction will be when two (or more) planets are in the same sign.

So, we could say the Sun and the Moon are conjunct in the sign of Scorpio at some point in November... as the Sun will enter Scorpio round about the 21st of October and the Moon travels through each sign every 28 days, so at some point in November they're bound to be in the same sign. If you want to check this out on the 7th and 8th of November 2018, the Sun and Moon will be in the sign of Scorpio.

And on those dates the Sun and Moon are conjunct...

In your birth chart, you could have any combination of planets conjunct. Your Sun could conjunct any of the other planets.
There are symbol shorthands for these aspects and the one for a conjunction looks like a teeny circle with a stick on it.

Here is a break down of the maths involved:

Angle: 0°
Division of circle by: 1
Keyword: Unifies

In our chart example Elizabeth had her Sun sign of Pisces conjunct her Mercury, Mars and Pluto, so those three planets were all in Pisces and all got along very well in her chart. They all understood each other. This means she felt it was easy to communicate deeply and doing so energised her. Also her Saturn and Uranus in Libra were also conjunct, meaning her sense of responsibility included ideas of freedom.

Trine
Another friendly aspect is the trine.
This is when two (or more) planets are about 120 degrees away from each other.
All the planets of the same Element are trine *to each other*.
As a reminder,
The Earth signs are Taurus, Virgo and Capricorn.
The Air signs are Gemini, Libra and Aquarius.
The Fire signs are Aries, Leo and Sagittarius.
The Water signs are Cancer and Scorpio Pisces.
Don't worry. You don't have to remember any of this coz it's all done for you. I'm just explaining it so you can get a grasp of why we call things the way we do and the reasoning behind it.

The symbol for a trine looks like a triangle and is one of the easiest to remember as trine and triangle have similar spelling.
Here is the maths:

Angle: 120°
Division of the circle by: 3
Keyword: Assists

In Robert's chart he had Sun in Taurus trine Saturn in Capricorn which are both Earth signs. So his ego-self was very friendly with his idea of authority and responsibility. And his Moon in Aries was trine his Uranus in Sagittarius which are both Fire signs, so in his case he truly needed emotional freedom.

Sextile

And lastly we have the sextile.
For some reason this is the one I always have trouble remembering the numbers of. But anyway, as it's another friendly one, see if you can identify if you've got any on your chart. Maybe I'd remember it better if I connected the word sextile with the letter S and the word six as it divides the circle into six bits. The symbol is easy enough to identify as it looks like a little star. Sextiles unite signs that are complimentary to each other across the qualities.
So Earth gets along with Water and Fire gets along with Air.

Here is the maths:
Angle: 60°
Division of the circle by: 6
Keyword: Supports

Elizabeth had Mercury and Mars in Pisces, a Water sign, sextile Jupiter in Capricorn, an Earth sign. So she wouldn't have had any difficulty between her thinking (Mercury) and beliefs (Jupiter) and might in fact have had belief in her thinking.

Don't Get Bogged Down

Please don't get bogged down with all of the mathematics involved, as it's very easy to get stuck in this thinking and completely lose touch with reality. I've witnessed far too many Astrologers getting all caught up in aspects and discussing in great detail one planet's attitude to another, when what we really need to do is keep in mind that we're learning about humans here, not robots.

Even if you had none of these aspects in your chart, it wouldn't matter as I'm sure you've got plenty of other chart features that can bring you joy. The secret is to seek them out, identify them and celebrate them!

In Elizabeth's chart she has, as we've discussed, Sun Pisces, Moon Libra with a Virgo Ascendant.
Sun Pisces is wildly romantic. Not in a practical way. They can very easily fall in love with love and make the whole love thing into something so unobtainable that they never actually experience it in one lifetime and have to get reincarnated again.
Her chart is very one-sided, so (unlike me!) she was fab at focusing on one thing at a time.
She had her Sun conjunct Pluto and Venus, which helped her to deeply drill down into how something felt for her (Pluto). She didn't just have feelings she had to completely and utterly experience them.

Lots of people have Sun conjunct Venus as Venus transits round about the same speed as the Sun so it's never more than one sign away from your Sun sign.

On the one hand her Moon in Libra wanted a relationship (Libra is the sign of relationships) while her Sun in Pisces wanted something deeply mysterious, upsetting and life-changing (Pluto) but loving and uplifting (Venus).

And as we know from their life-story, she did the ultimate thing by 'sacrificing' her contact with her dad to 'run-away' with the man who worked very, very hard to win her over.

Being a poet fulfilled a lot of her needs too. All those long, detailed writings kept her Virgo Ascendant busy and her Sun in the 6th was good at focusing. She not only wrote poems, she wrote hundreds of letters.

Sometimes daily.

She was confined mostly to her room in the family house because of her health, so she had plenty of time to write. Also, her father's reluctance to deal with the death of his wife, and his daughters' (he had more than one) future independence meant he actively *encouraged* his daughters to stay-away-from-men.

Robert (possibly) had a Sagittarius Ascendant - enjoying foreign travel, higher education and learning, Sun in Taurus: loving life's luxuries and a need for stability, with Moon in Aries: emotionally honest, capable of flare-ups but not resentful.

His Venus in Cancer is conjunct Jupiter in Cancer, making his love needs bigger than they might be. Jupiter always adds extra zoompf to a conjunction. It exaggerates and magnifies whatever planet it's next to.

His chart is a See Saw, so he swung from one thing to another.
His Sun sign is also (probably) in the 6th house so, like Elizabeth, detail and being exact were important to him.

Between their two charts there are some nice, friendly aspects, which we will discuss in more detail in chapter six.

Finding the positive parts of your chart will really help bolster your confidence and allow you to avoid any romantic pitfalls.

Keep focused on those good points.

Remind yourself continually you possess them and they will bless your present relationship or any you might find in the future.

Chapter Five

Using Astrology to Discover the Optimum Time to Meet 'The One'

Astrology is very useful when it comes to finding the best time to 'do' something. Assuming of course that you have a choice about timing. Sometimes you can meet someone when you least expect it, and everything progresses happily.

However, people that haven't met 'The One' yet wonder: *'Is there a good time or a bad time to be out there looking*?'

Well, there's no good or bad time, as Astrology can't be divided into good or bad. It's better to think about when the optimum time to be looking, dating, searching or thinking might be. And that *can* be discovered.

So far we've discussed how to make a chart and how to find out what your love needs are.

We've looked at and discussed lovers that have made it past the first hurdle of meeting 'The One' so how do you do that too?

The birth chart is static. It doesn't change, which is good as otherwise life would be very difficult for Astrologers!

What *does* change is the location and position of the planets before and after your birth. In fact they change every minute of every day.

Transits

A transit is Astrology-Speak for a planet's movement.

The Moon is moving at a rate of approximately 13 degrees through each sign of the Zodiac (each sign is 30 degrees) every day and then changes sign from one sign to the next every 2 days or so. It actually takes 28 days for it to go through all the signs of the Zodiac from Aries to Pisces so while you're reading this it will be moving.

So, even though your chart stays the same, at any point in time, the planets continue to move in their orbits and Astrologers call this movement a 'transit'.

So we'd say something like: *'Uranus is transiting her natal Mars in Aries'* meaning in their birth chart they've got Mars in the sign of Aries... and at this precise moment in time, Uranus is *also* in the sign of Aries so those two planets are meeting each other. The birth planet in your chart is being aspected by the transit of Uranus.

Remembering of course that all transits of planets affect everyone, some people more than others.

Say you've got Moon in Libra and just at this moment Jupiter has started to travel through the sign of Libra, which it will take one year to do. That movement will send a little message to your birth chart. Now, there is no way of proving this. I don't have 'evidence' of this movement today affecting something from when you're born.
You can think of it like this:

Imagine you're at the wedding of a work friend.

There you are, standing with your work colleagues. Lots of people are wandering around you, walking past you but not stopping and talking to you. Some are women. Some are men. Some are kiddies. All sorts of different people.

Then you notice someone on the other side of the room who is wearing *exactly the same outfit* as you. However, they're a different size to you.
A bit larger. Taller. Louder than you.

That outfit represents the *sign* of the Zodiac that your Moon is in (Libra)
Maybe the outfit is a gentle pastel colour.

They've got the same *sign* Libra (outfit) as you but *their* planet is Jupiter, which is a much bigger planet than the Moon.

Now Jupiter and the Moon get along quite well in Astrology so the Jupiter/Larger person is far more likely to come over and talk to you and say something like 'Snap!' and start a conversation.

It's a bit like that in Astrology.

All the time planets are orbiting, going past the place they were when you were born and at certain times of year, certain planets (there are 10 we take into account in a chart) will align exactly with your birth planets. Some of those alignments will make your birth chart (and you) feel happy and some will make you feel sad/confused/upset. What we want to find out is when those positive transits will occur, so you're more likely to be optimising the best times to actively seek love.

The planets that make the most impact are the ones we discussed in Chapter Two: Venus and Mars as they're the love planets.

So go to www.astro.com and find out what signs those two planets are in today and using their Ephemeris, calculate when they're going to be in compatible signs to yours.

Here's the link:
http://www.astro.com/swisseph/swepha_e.htm

Or go to www.astro.com.
Click on All About Astrology.
Then click on 9000 Years Ephemeris
The choose 21st century for the years 2000 to 2099
Then choose what year you want to explore.
Each year is saved as a PDF, which you can download.
It will have all the months of the year on it, and each day of the year's planets going from the Sun-Pluto.
It is written in Astrological code, so make sure you know your planet and sign symbols before you try to make sense of this!

Reminder:

This is the symbol for Venus

This is the symbol for Mars

I'll use an example here.

Julie is a Sun Sign Sagittarius, with Venus in Scorpio and Mars in Sagittarius.
On the date I gave her some advice, Mars was already in the sign of Sagittarius and Venus went into Scorpio on the 24th of that month. Super! Ideal time for Julie to be dating was NOW!

The signs that get along better with each other are the same Elements, as we discussed in Chapter Two.

Remember, Earth gets along well with Water.

And Air gets along well with Fire.

The Earth signs are: Taurus, Virgo and Capricorn.
The Air signs are: Gemini, Libra and Aquarius.
The Water signs are: Cancer, Scorpio and Pisces.
The Fire signs are: Aries, Leo and Sagittarius.

Find out when Venus and Mars are going to be in either the exact signs of your birth chart (like in Julie's chart) or in ones that will be in the same or compatible Elements.
When you do this exercise, you'll discover that there are some months and dates that are better than others.
On the months where the planets are working for you, make sure you're actively seeking romance.

On the months they're not, concentrate on your social dating profile if you're dating on-line. Or go out with friends. Un-focus from active-partner-seeking and settle into receiving mode.

The reason I suggest this is because on the months when the planets aren't playing ball with your chart, they could be doing fab things for your intended's chart!

It's not just all about you, this looking-for-love business. The person you're trying to find might also be trying to find you! There are two energies at work! So don't drive yourself crazy and exhaust your love-drive.

I found, over the years, that February for some strange reason was when most of my relationships started. I never even thought about it, until I was older. Then I realised that during February, Venus and Mars were transiting through the sign of Aquarius, which is the sign of *my* Venus *and* Mars. So even though I never used Astrology consciously, Astrology was guiding my love-life!

If you're extremely impatient (are you a Fire sign by any chance?) and you don't want to wait for a Venus or Mars transit, you can do the same exercise with the Moon.

As the Moon only takes 28 days to go through the whole of the Zodiac's signs, there will be at least 2 days every month where your chances are optimised.

And if your Venus and Mars are in different signs, even better! There will be 4 days in every 28 when you're maximising your reach.

Elizabeth and Robert's First Contact

So, when did Elizabeth and Robert first meet?
Their first contact chart is very interesting. This is a
chart made for the exact date that Elizabeth received
her first letter from him. Don't forget, at this stage
she had not met him, or he her. But they did have a
mutual friend.

Reminder:
Elizabeth has Sun Pisces, Moon Virgo, Venus and
Mars in Pisces.

Robert has Sun Taurus, Moon Aries, Venus Cancer,
Mars Gemini and possibly (we don't know for sure) a
Sagittarius Ascendant.

On the date she received the letter, Venus was in
Sagittarius, Mars was in Scorpio and the Moon and
Neptune were in friendship-loving Aquarius.

The chart opposite shows how that was from
Elizabeth's point of view.

Her chart is in the middle, the outer ring contains the
planets on the day she received the letter and on the
outside are the signs of the Zodiac.

The Moon and Neptune were transiting her 5th house
of romance.

Jupiter was transiting her Venus and was just about
to transit into her 7th house of marriage.

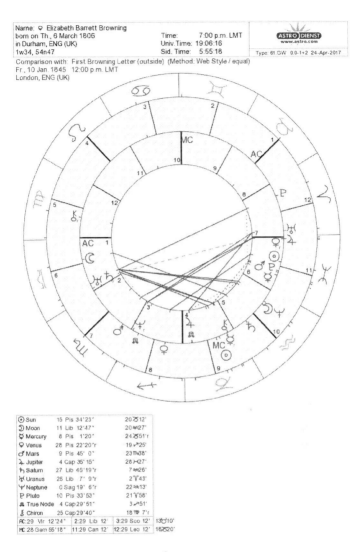

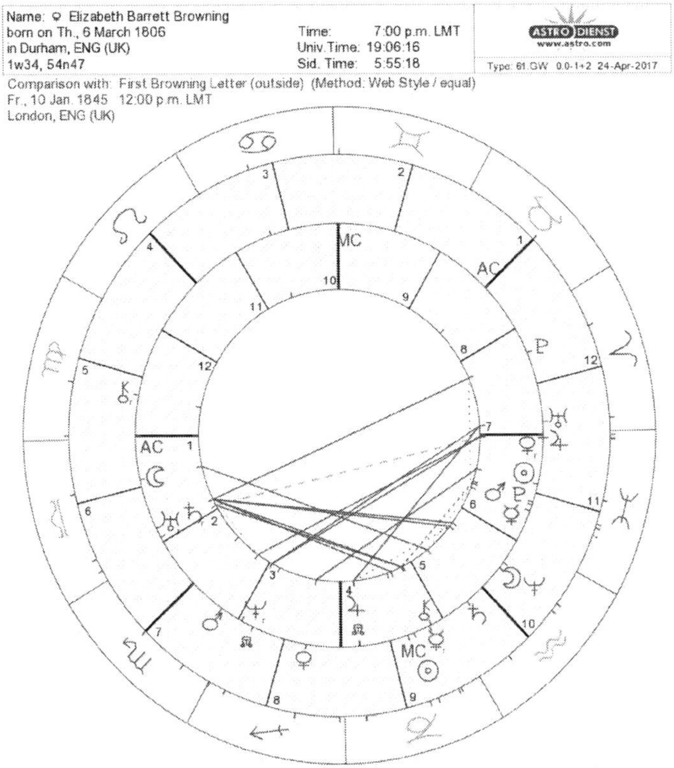
Name: ♀ Elizabeth Barrett Browning
born on Th., 6 March 1806
in Durham, ENG (UK)
1w34, 54n47
Time: 7:00 p.m. LMT
Univ.Time: 19:06:16
Sid. Time: 5:55:18
ASTRODIENST
www.astro.com
Type: 61.GW 0.0-1+2 24-Apr-2017
Comparison with: First Browning Letter (outside) (Method: Web Style / equal)
Fr., 10 Jan. 1845 12:00 p.m. LMT
London, ENG (UK)
MC
AC

☉ Sun	15 Pis 34'23"	20♉12'
☽ Moon	11 Lib 12'47"	20♒27'
☿ Mercury	8 Pis 1'20"	24♉51'r
♀ Venus	28 Pis 22'20"r	19♐25'
♂ Mars	9 Pis 45' 0"	23♏38'
♃ Jupiter	4 Cap 35'15"	28♓27'
♄ Saturn	27 Lib 46'19"r	7♒26'
♅ Uranus	25 Lib 7' 9"r	2♈43'
♆ Neptune	0 Sag 19' 6"r	22♒13'
♇ Pluto	10 Pis 33'53"	21♈58'
☊ True Node	4 Cap 29'51"	3♐51'
⚷ Chiron	25 Cap 29'40"	18♍ 7'r

AC: 29 Vir 12'24"	2: 29 Lib 12'	3: 29 Sco 12'	13♉10'
MC: 28 Gem 55'18"	11: 29 Can 12'	12: 29 Leo 12'	18♉20'

Figure 2

Now, this wasn't any ordinary letter that Robert wrote. Remember he's a poet and so is Elizabeth, so his first letter was about their mutual writing.

Here's a little segment of it:

*'I love your verses with all my heart, dear Miss
Barrett, - and this is no off-hand complimentary
letter that I shall write, - whatever else, no prompt
matter-of-course recognition of your genius, and
there a graceful and natural end of the thing.
Since the day last week when I first read your
poems, I quite laugh to remember how I have been
turning and turning again in my mind what I
should be able to tell you of their effect upon me, for
in the first flush of delight I thought I would this
once get out of my habit of purely passive
enjoyment, when I do really enjoy, and thoroughly
justify my admiration - perhaps even, as a loyal
fellow-craftsman should, try and find fault and do
you some little good to be proud hereafter! - but
nothing comes of it all - so into me has it gone, and
part of me has it become, this great living poetry of
yours, not a flower of which but took root and
grew...'*[13]

In this first letter, he compliments Elizabeth on her
poetry (he had copies of her poetry books), tells her
how instead of writing to criticise her poems, they
have made a deep impression on him and have gone
deeply into him and 'taken root'.

He also said, and this was the decider, I expect: *'I do,
as I say, love these books with all my heart - and I
love you too. Do you know I was once not very far
from seeing - really seeing you?'*

Elizabeth Replies – Fast!

Elizabeth didn't waste any time replying. That same day she replied to him writing a 650-word letter, which he received the next day.

She told him she'd like to know any *'faults as rise to the surface and strike you as important in my poems'*, and that she had *'high respect for your power in your Art'* and questioned was it *'indeed true that I was so near to the pleasure and honour of making your acquaintance?'* as he'd mentioned in his letter that he'd nearly met her a while ago. This was via a mutual friend of theirs.

The writing continued for the rest of that year and into the next and eventually they met up, got married and 'ran away' to live in Italy.

John Lennon and Yoko Ono's First Meet-Up

John Lennon and Yoko Ono's first meeting was slightly less romantic. John is no longer living, however there is a lovely video recording on YouTube from 1969 where John and Yoko were interviewed on the David Frost Show. John tells the story of how they met.

Yoko was hosting an Art exhibition where she was asking participants to bang a nail into a piece of wood. She'd already been briefed that he was a rich musician from a famous band called The Beatles. In the interview he tells what happened when Yoko says: *'OK, you can hammer a nail in for five shillings.'* John continues:

'So smartass says, "Well, I'll give you an imaginary five shillings and hammer an imaginary nail in." And that's when we really met. That's when we locked eyes and she got it and I got it and, as they say in all the interviews we do, the rest is history.'

If the date recorded is correct, the transits for that date were: the Sun, Venus and Neptune were in Scorpio, and the Moon, Mars, Uranus and Pluto were all in Virgo.

Reminder
Yoko has Libra Ascendant, Sun in Aquarius, Moon in Sagittarius, Venus in Aquarius and Mars in Virgo. John has Aries Ascendant, Sun in Libra, Moon in Aquarius, Venus in Virgo and Mars in Libra.

As both Yoko and John have Virgo Love planets: Mars and Venus, the Moon (emotions), Mars (action), Uranus (sudden happenings) and Pluto (deep change) were all triggering off Yoko's Mars and John's Venus as they were in the same signs.
Even if that date is not correct, the outer planets transiting that year (it's a definite they met that year), were Jupiter (belief), which was in the sign of Leo and was transiting conjunct John's Pluto (deep change).
Jupiter was also opposite both Yoko's Sun in Aquarius and John's Moon in Aquarius.
Astrologically this was a meaningful time for them, something they wouldn't forget easily.

Mid and Outer Planets
Other planets can also have an effect on your birth Astrology during the beginning of a relationship.

Jupiter helps make the beginning active, international and/or philosophical.

Saturn helps make the relationship serious.

Uranus makes it exciting and/or exhausting.

Neptune can either make it a soul-connection or deluded.

Pluto can make it dramatic and deeply transformative or draining.

These transits will aspect your chart in some way. Maybe they're conjunct (right next to) your Ascendant, your Sun, Moon, Venus or Mars.
I checked back to my own dating history and my first (long-term) relationship started when Saturn was conjunct my Ascendant.
My first marriage relationship started when Venus and Mars were conjunct my Sun.
My second marriage relationship started when Saturn was conjunct my Moon.

These transits happen all the time to all of us, and if we pay attention to when they're doing nice things with our chart, then we're working with the energies of the planets and are more likely to hit lucky.

Asking the Universe for Help
Something that will really help your ability to meet and date with The One is to write a letter to the universe asking for help. This is something that I recommend to all of my clients because it is easy to do. All you need is a piece of paper and pen.
I hasten to add that this isn't an Astrological suggestion. This comes from my own personal experience.
Have a think about the qualities you'd like your ideal mate to possess.
Do you want them to love you unconditionally?
Do you want them to be faithful? Gentle? Exciting? Playful? Honest?
Then the practical stuff:

To live near you.

Be solvent.

Or have the same level of education.

Be thoughtful about your decisions, as once you've written your letter you'll be provided with what you asked for...

As we discussed in other chapters, make sure you ask for what you *want*, not what you don't want.

Be clear.

Be positive.

Write things like: *'must be teetotal'* not: *'I don't want an alcoholic'*

Remember to include things like domestic arrangements.

Children.

Do you want to marry?

And if not marry, how will you want to celebrate your union?

Once you've given some thought to the things you know you truly want, write them on one side of A4 paper... then fold the paper in 4, burn it... and let it go...

Now, if you're a little unsure about whether or not your letter to the Universe will work and would prefer some extra help, I developed a wonderful Homeopathic remedy (accidently) in 1999 that helps draw your Soul Mate/The One/Life Partner to you. It's called Tempesta and you can read more about it on my website here:

https://www.maryenglish.com/stormremedy01.html

and here:

http://www.maryenglish.com/tempesta.html

Helios the homeopathic pharmacy sells it or you can order it direct from me.

Email mary@maryenglish.com for more info.

Chapter Six

Astrological Methods to Check Your Compatibility Using Synastry and Composite charts

There are various ways you can check your compatibility. I will start with the easiest and work up to the more difficult. Please remember, as always, there is no point using any of these methods if there is no chance that Mr or Miss Right will reciprocate your affections.

As I mentioned earlier, I have an ancient computer programme that calculates as a percentage how compatible I can be with other people.

The question is, do you want to know your compatibility as a number?

Or an explanation?

What do you view compatibility as?

Finding the same things interesting?

My faithful dictionary describes compatible as: *Able to coexist (with); mutually tolerant.*

Coexisting

That's a useful idea to keep in mind: if you're going to spend the rest of your life with someone, or at the very least a few years, being able to coexist is a must. However, there are as many different types of relationships as there are stars in the sky.

What you need to find out is, what *you* classify as important to you.

Astrology already knows which signs of the Zodiac get along better with others.

I still think it's strange how that really hasn't changed over hundreds of years. If you ever look back in history, you can find out who got along better with whom just by their Sun signs...

An easy way to remember compatibility is that each sign of the Zodiac gets along better with every *other* sign.

If you were to line all the signs up from Aries to Pisces and counted not the sign next to yours, but the sign *afterwards* as your compatible sign, you'd find the best match.

That's a simple, easy way to remember compatibility.

So, start with your sign, skip one, the next sign is compatible, skip one... and so on...
For instance: Aries gets along better with Gemini, Leo, Libra, Sagittarius and Aquarius but finds Taurus, Cancer, Virgo etc challenging.

Taurus gets along better with Cancer, Virgo, Scorpio, Capricorn and Pisces but finds Gemini, Leo, Libra, Sagittarius, Aquarius and Aries challenging.

Don't panic if your nearest and dearest is supposedly incompatible!

There will be something linking your two charts. Maybe your Ascendants get along fine, or your Moons are nice and friendly to each other.

Synastry Charts

I use this method the most. For me, it's the easiest to quickly work out which parts of Ms A's chart is good-to-go with Mr B's.

Here's how to do it.

You'll need an Astrological computer programme or the Internet site www.astro.com
I'm sure there are many other sites out there, but I don't use them so I'm not going to recommend them as so few sites will use Equal house. Equal House is the easiest house system to use and the one of the oldest and to my thinking: if it ain't broke, don't fix it.

Once you've made your account, go to the extended chart section, which comes under Drawings and Calculations.
Horoscope for:
Partner:

For this we are going to use our chart examples of Elizabeth and Robert.
Birth data is:
Elizabeth 6th March 1806, 7pm Killoe, England
Robert 7th May 1812 10pm Camberwell, England

N.B. Robert's time of birth has no accurate reference and was estimated by a family history researcher.

Elizabeth and Robert

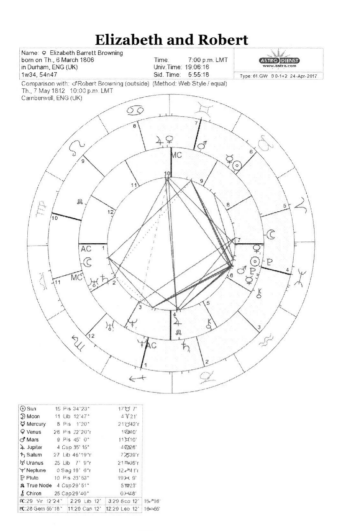

Name: ♀ Elizabeth Barrett Browning
born on Th., 6 March 1806
in Durham, ENG (UK)
1w34, 54n47

Time: 7:00 p.m. LMT
Univ.Time: 19:06:16
Sid. Time: 5:55:18

Type: 61.GW 0 0-1+2 24-Apr-2017

ASTRO DIENST
www.astro.com

Comparison with: ♂Robert Browning (outside) (Method: Web Style / equal)
Th., 7 May 1812 10:00 p.m. LMT
Camberwell, ENG (UK)

⊙ Sun	15 Pis 34'23"	17 ♉ 7'	
☽ Moon	11 Lib 12'47"	4 ♈21'	
☿ Mercury	8 Pis 1'20"	21 ♉42' r	
♀ Venus	28 Pis 22'20" r	1 ♊40'	
♂ Mars	9 Pis 45' 0"	11 ♓10'	
♃ Jupiter	4 Cap 35' 15"	4 ♋26'	
♄ Saturn	27 Lib 46'19" r	7 ♏39' r	
♅ Uranus	25 Lib 7' 9" r	21 ♏06' r	
♆ Neptune	0 Sag 19' 6" r	12 ♐41' r	
♇ Pluto	10 Pis 33'53"	19 ♓ 9'	
☊ True Node	4 Cap 29' 51"	5 ♊23'	
⚷ Chiron	25 Cap 29'40"	0 ♈48'	
AC: 29 Vir 12'24"	2:29 Lib 12'	3:29 Sco 12'	15 ♐16'
MC: 28 Gem 55'18"	11:29 Can 12'	12:29 Leo 12'	16 ♎55'

Figure 3

When you do this for your own charts, remember who you put in first as that's the chart that will be in the centre.
The signs of the Zodiac go round the outside of the wheel.

Whoever you choose first, will be the 'starting chart' and the wheel will start in the sign of the Ascendant of that person.

So, in our lovers' Synastry chart, Elizabeth is the lead chart, and Robert the outside chart and the joint chart starts in the sign of Virgo.

Chart Shape

Now, the first thing you need to look for is chart shape.

Is everything bundled together or are the respective planets dotted around the circle?

Does it look busy or empty or just right?

What's always nice to see is when one person's planets fill in the gaps of the other person's chart. So between them, they have more combined signs and maybe the two of them coming together then have a better understanding of 'others'.

If you and your intended have all your planets in the same place, or very near together, watch out for getting too stuck in a groove.

As you can see in this example, Elizabeth doesn't have any planets in the signs of Aries, Taurus, Gemini or Cancer but Robert does. So he added those signs' energies into her life. Nice!

He doesn't have any planets in Libra and she does, so maybe she brought some balance and beauty into his life?

She also has a bunch of planets in Pisces: Sun, Mercury, Venus, Mars and Pluto and he only has Pluto in Pisces ... so again, she brought some of that Pisces fantasy into his life. The shared Pluto was a bit tricky as his Pluto rested almost exactly on her Sun, which might have made her feel he was a bit forceful or controlling of her...

As Elizabeth's chart is so one-sided, it was nice that Robert brought a little bit of balance to her chart by giving her another perspective on life. She'd spent a long amount of years, in her room, not venturing out until Robert appeared in her life. She was almost a prisoner of her father who demanded that she and her sisters were 'never to marry' and was also deeply affected by the death of her mother and later her brother.

She was quite a sensitive lady.

Elizabeth and Robert's Child

After a number of miscarriages, Elizabeth gave birth to a son they called Robert Wiedeman Barrett Browning but nicknamed 'Pen'. He had the same Sun and Moon as his mother, Sun Pisces, Moon Virgo and he married an heiress called Fannie who was a Virgo.

They had no children.

Yoko and John

Name: ♀ Yoko Ono
born on Sa, 18 February 1933
in Tokyo, JAPAN
139e46, 35n42

Time: 8:30 p.m.
Univ.Time: 11:30
Sid. Time: 6:40:58

ASTRO·DIENST
www.astro.com
Type: 61 GW 0 0-1+2 24-Apr-2017

Comparison with: ♂ John Lennon (outside) (Method: Web Style / equal)
We., 9 Oct. 1940   6:30 p.m.
Liverpool, ENG (UK)

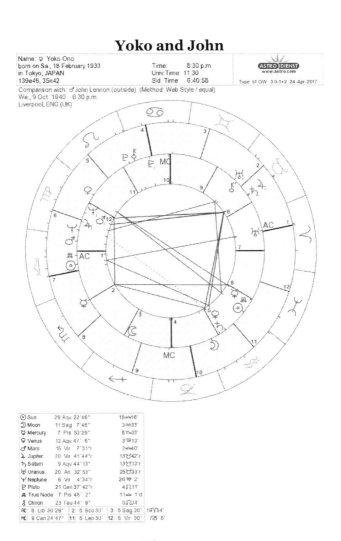

☉ Sun	29 Aqu 22'46"	18♒16'	
☽ Moon	11 Sag 7'46"	3♒33'	
☿ Mercury	7 Pis 53'29"	8♏33'	
♀ Venus	13 Aqu 47' 6"	3♍13'	
♂ Mars	15 Vir 7'31"r	2♋40'	
♃ Jupiter	20 Vir 41'44"r	13♉42'r	
♄ Saturn	9 Aqu 44'13"	13♉13'r	
♅ Uranus	20 Ari 32'53"	25♉33'r	
♆ Neptune	9 Vir 4'34"r	26♍ 2'	
♇ Pluto	21 Can 37'42"r	4♌11'	
☊ True Node	7 Pis 48' 2"	11♎ 1'd	
⚷ Chiron	23 Tau 44' 9"	0♌24'	
AC: 8 Lib 30'29"	2: 6 Sco 30'	3: 8 Sag 30'	19♈54'
MC: 9 Can 24'47"	11: 6 Leo 30'	12: 8 Vir 30'	7♉ 6'

Figure 4

In Yoko and John's charts, their chart shape is more
Splay. Planets all around the circle but clustered into
little clumps. Yoko is on the inside, John on the
outside.

Between the two of them, they cover all the signs of the Zodiac except Capricorn: the sign of sensible pragmatism, and Gemini the sign of the communicator.

They have 9 fixed planets, 7 mutable, 4 cardinal planets so their combined chart is predominantly fixed, not wanting or liking change.

(See page 6 for more info on cardinal, fixed and mutable).

Yoko still lives in the New York City apartment they were living in when John was murdered. When asked by an interviewer if she'd ever think about moving she replied:

'Never. We shared this every day. Every day we shared each room. I wouldn't do that.'

So it isn't a tragic place?

'The good memory supersedes the bad memory. The bad memory was just one that was terrible. But other than that, I felt we were still together. I would feel very strange if I had to leave this apartment. There are so many things that he touched here that he loved. Those things mean a lot.'[14]

As they also have very few cardinal planets, they weren't that concerned about the future and with 7 mutable planets their relationship was focused in the past.

The biggest connection is how John's Sun and Mars sandwich Yoko's Ascendant.

When someone's Sun or other personal planet connects with your Ascendant it will be hard to ignore the effect.

Notice also how John's Ascendant connects exactly with Yoko's Uranus in her 7th House of marriage. It really would be quite difficult to ignore that sort of connection with your 7th house! In their case, as we know, they didn't ignore it and became a couple very quickly after that first in-person meeting.

John's Children

John's children are Julian, who is a Sun Aries, Moon Libra from John's first marriage to Cynthia who has Virgo Sun, Leo Moon.
Sean, the child of Yoko and John, is a Sun Libra, Moon Sagittarius. As you can see, there is a Libra theme running through their family history.

In the next set of charts we're going to learn a little about some clients of mine...

Real-Life Example

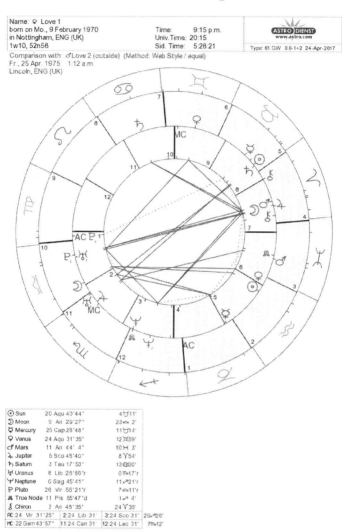

Name: ♀ Love 1
born on Mo., 9 February 1970
in Nottingham, ENG (UK)
1w10, 52n58

Time: 9:15 p.m.
Univ.Time: 20:15
Sid. Time: 5:28:21

ASTRO DIENST
www.astro.com

Type: 61.GW 0.0-1+2 24-Apr-2017

Comparison with: ♂ Love 2 (outside) (Method: Web Style / equal)
Fr., 25 Apr. 1975 1:12 a.m.
Lincoln, ENG (UK)

☉ Sun	20 Aqu 40'44"	4 ♉ 11'		
☽ Moon	9 Ari 29'27"	23 ♒ 2'		
☿ Mercury	25 Cap 28'48"	11 ♉ 14'		
♀ Venus	24 Aqu 31'35"	12 ♓ 59'		
♂ Mars	11 Ari 44' 4"	10 ♓ 3'		
♃ Jupiter	5 Sco 48'40"	8 ♈ 54'		
♄ Saturn	3 Tau 17'53"	13 ♋ 30'		
♅ Uranus	6 Lib 25'56"r	0 ♍ 17'r		
♆ Neptune	0 Sag 45'41"	11 ♐ 21'r		
♇ Pluto	26 Vir 55'21"r	7 ♏ 11'r		
♏ True Node	11 Pis 55'47"d	1 ♐ 4'		
⚷ Chiron	3 Ari 48'35"	24 ♈ 35'		
AC: 24 Vir 31'25"	2:24 Lib 31'	3:24 Sco 31'	29 ♐ 26'	
MC: 22 Gem 43'57"	11:24 Can 31'	12:24 Leo 31'	7 ♏ 12'	

Figure 5

Catherine and Doug

'My partner and I have been together for over 5 years now, we're not married but we do have a fantastic relationship. We also do have our ups and downs but somehow we are very equipped to get through the tough times. I have looked at our synastry chart over the years and the pair of us do have some aspects that bind us.'

In this relationship here are the key points. There is a 5-year age gap between them and they're both born in the 1970s.

Catherine has:
Ascendant Virgo Mutable/Earth
Sun Aquarius Fixed/Air in the 5th house
Moon Aries Cardinal/Fire in the 7th house
Venus Aquarius Fixed/Air
Mars Aries Cardinal/Fire

Doug has:
Ascendant Sagittarius Mutable/Fire
Sun Taurus Fixed/Air in the 5th house
Moon Libra Cardinal/Air in the 5th house
Venus Gemini Mutable/Air
Mars Pisces Mutable/Water

Both their Ascendants are Mutable. Both their Sun signs are Fixed. Both of their Moons are Cardinal so on the face of it there is a lot of attraction. However, Doug's Mars in Pisces really won't 'do' it for Catherine and she might find that she nags him to be more of a 'man' as Mars in Pisces is a very sensitive placement. I've not found many relationships that have lasted for long with that without lots of work. The other thing that could be proving stressful for Catherine is she was born with Moon and Mars conjunct opposition Uranus. And if you look carefully at their Synastry chart you'll see that Doug's Pluto is exactly conjunct Catherine's Uranus... so not only does she now (when they're together) have Moon opposition Uranus (a needing for complete emotional freedom) but with Doug's Pluto also in the mix, she's going to feel quite a lot of the time disempowered.

There's another interesting feature of their combined charts. This is using the methods Judy Hall describes in her wonderful book *Hands Across Time* where she discusses past life experiences between couples.

Saturn is a male parenting planet and the Sun is male.

Catherine has Saturn in Taurus and Doug has Sun in Taurus, so in a past life, Catherine was Doug's father and he was her son. Reincarnating and having a personal *romantic* relationship with someone who you (might) have had a parenting past life with, can be tricky.
The lesson they need to learn in this lifetime is that freedom is important but also so is intimacy and gentleness.

Hopefully Doug's Mars in Pisces can have nice, friendly conversations with Catherine's Jupiter in Scorpio.

While Doug's Jupiter in Aries can 'teach' Catherine's Mars and Moon in her 7th house, that if you believe a relationship will last... it will.

Now, because they're both Fixed signs, they're less likely to want to walk away from this relationship. Plus Doug has Moon in Libra, which gets along very well with Catherine's Sun in Aquarius as they're both Air signs. So, providing they can *talk* about how they *feel* and negotiate (which incidentally all people in relationships must do) then they will continue to grow and blossom.

Synastry charts are great fun to make. You don't have to just use them for potential or newly acquired partners, they can also be used to check how you get along with other members of your family, or your friends.

I always use the centre or first chart of the person I am SURE I have correct data for.

That way, I can make an accurate analysis of the energies between both people and because the Ascendant is known, I can find out what might have been the initial attraction.

Ascendant Attraction

The Ascendant sign (which can be any sign of the Zodiac depending on time of birth) will determine how quickly you will be attracted to, or attracted by potential partners.

At the beginning of a relationship most people operate through their Ascending sign.

And as most people are on their 'best behaviour' when they first start to date, knowing the Ascending sign will give you an edge of understanding.

When stressed, or under pressure, most people react like their Ascending sign, rather than their Sun sign. As birth is pretty stressful (in a good way) you will always return to that sign's *modus operandi,* when you hit the stress and excitement of new love.

Be careful if you fall in love *only* with someone's Ascending sign. It's very easy to do but will cause heaps of problems later on, if your Sun signs aren't compatible.

It is *not* who they are. It's just how they project themselves.

My first husband and I had very compatible Ascendants. His is Sagittarius and mine is Leo, so those two Fire signs caused lots of sparks.

However, after 10 years together and one baby, he found a deeper love with someone whose Sun sign was far more compatible with his than mine.

Composite Charts

A Composite chart is a bit more complex. It involves merging the two charts together by using a thing called a Mid-Point.

A Mid-Point is the exact middle point/degree between two planets.

Say I have Sun in Pisces (which I do) 15 degrees and Mr Magic has Sun in Cancer 15 degrees, then the exact Mid-Point between our two Suns would be Taurus 15 degrees.

Don't event attempt to make this chart up yourself. We'll do it using the website.(like in Julie's chart) Here's how we do it.

Go to www.astro.com

Place your curser over Free Horoscopes and a little section will open up Daily Horoscopes, Short Horoscopes etc,
Move your curser over to the right to the section marked Drawings and Calculations and click on the section marked Extended Chart Selection.

Birth Data
On this birth data page, enter all the date/time/location information.
There will be two boxes:
Horoscope for:
Partner:

Choose which two charts you want to use to create the composite.
Make sure it says circular charts in red (it should do as that's the default)
Methods: Circular charts | Special charts | Ephemeris | Pullen/Astrolog

Chart type

On this box choose Composite Chart, Midpoint-method (2)
The box underneath says:

Chart drawing style

Leave that as default

Options
Under options, which is a little further down the page, look at:
House System
Click and choose equal
Then click the blue button 'click here to show chart'

Now, if you've done this correctly it should say at the top left of your chart the name and birth data in black of person number one and the name and birth data of person number two in red.

You will now have a totally new chart. This chart represents your relationship. What the two of you together creates. It's a totally new entity. You're not separate beings anymore, you're what you'd be Astrologically if half of you was stuck onto half of someone else.

Using the Synastry method we were looking at how each chart got along with the other.

With the Composite method we've created a chart to represent the relationship itself.
Cool!

The first thing (as always) that we will need to pay attention to is the Ascendant.

What sign and Element is it?

Elizabeth and Robert Composite

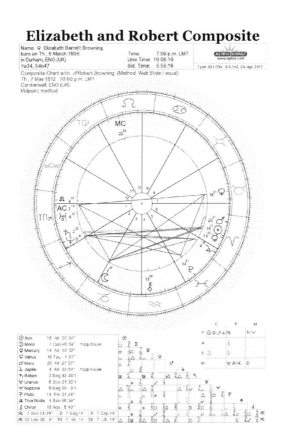

Figure 6

In our love example, Elizabeth and Robert's Composite chart has a Scorpio Ascendant, which I think describes very well their relationship to the outside world. It appeared secretive (it had to be or it never would have happened!) and passionate. Well Robert seemed to exemplify that part. His poetry took on a new dimension when they met. With Uranus on the Ascendant, liberation and freedom were very important to them.

107

Their combined Sun sign is Aries, with Mars, Mercury and Jupiter in Aries too. After they married they became quite feisty. Writing poems about Italian politics, socialising with other poets and writers. Their combined Sun is located in the 6th house of health and work and they did work together. Very well.

Their combined Moon is in Capricorn in the 3rd, helping them be stoic communicators. And with Venus in stable Taurus in the 7th, there is no doubt that their relationship was true-love and steady.

This chart is not about how well you get along with someone. It's completely different to that. It represents the relationship that the two of you have created. That relationship only exists because the two of you are together. This is the Astrological equivalent of making a cake. The cake ingredients exist in their own right, before you make the cake. Then when all the ingredients are combined and cooked (or not, if you're into raw foods) they result in a cake. A totally different experience to the ingredients.

If you want a free analysis of your Composite charts, www.astro.com does have it.
Go to Free Horoscopes, then scroll your curser to Interactive Horoscopes and click on AstroClick Partner.
On this page, choose your charts and learn about your Composite planets and their locations, but again, you'll be using the Placidus system, so the houses will be in different sizes compared to Equal House. But don't worry it will give you enough useful information to learn a bit about your relationship.

Chapter Seven

The Problems
And Some Suggested Solutions

Problems in relationships happen when expectations are not met.

Bill expects Jane to make his breakfast everyday, but Jane is a freedom-loving Aquarius and hates routine or being at someone else's beck and call, whereas Bill is a traditional Taurus, loves his food and likes routine. There will certainly have to be some discussion to make this relationship work well.

Maybe Bill can make his own breakfast. Or maybe Jane could make breakfast for both of them at weekends. Without discussion, no-one will reach the place of love-nirvana.

Another problem people have is when one partner doesn't feel heard or understood.

To resolve this issue, we need to look at the sign their Mercury is in, as this represents how we communicate.

Mercury the Planet of Communication.
The Speedy Planet

Mercury is a funny little planet. It has a very erratic orbit. Sometimes it can be seen in the morning, sometimes in the evening. Goodness knows how the ancient Babylonians saw it, as it's not easy to see even with a telescope.

In our solar system it's the planet that is closest to the Sun. This makes its surface boiling hot in places, and freezing cold in others, as because of its orbit round the Sun only part of the planet actually faces the Sun. Bit like standing in front of a bonfire on a cold winter's night. If you're facing the fire, your front can get hot, but your back can get really chilly.

Mercury's orbit around the Sun is four times as fast as the Earth's, so its year is only 88 Earth days long. However, it spins so slowly on its axis that one day on Mercury is equal to 59 days on Earth. It is also the smallest planet in our solar system and is not so easy to spot; the best times being early evening in the spring and early morning in the autumn in the northern hemisphere.[15]

NASA's Messenger Probe

The American space agency NASA sent a probe called Messenger to explore the planet in 2004 and it became the first spacecraft to orbit the innermost planet on 18th March 2011. It was going to cease its investigations in March 2012, but secured funding for additional years of research.

It eventually finished its mission before crashing onto Mercury's surface on April 30, 2015.

There is another mission planned for Mercury, called BepiColombo, starting in 2018, organised by the European Space Agency and it's due to arrive in 2024. It will carry two orbiters, one from Europe and one from Japan.

So far they have discovered that the surface of Mercury is covered in volcanic explosions, craters and evidence of flood volcanism. The mission discovered water-ice in those craters.

The surface temperature is of two extremes. On the sunny side it reaches 430° C and on the dark side of the planet it goes into deep freeze with temperatures to a low -180° C. Hmm, don't fancy living there!

Mercury the Go-Between

If we look at Mercury in our solar system, we see that it stands between the Sun and us and I agree with Christina Rose who writes in her *Astrological Counselling*:

> Mercury, positioned closest to the Sun, stands rather as one who introduces the solar energy to all the other planets, and vice versa. Thus, his function is that of an introductory link, transmission, connection and we may liken Mercury to a go-between, an agent or courier between the Sun and the rest of the solar system. On an incoming wavelength, this function is experienced within the individual as recognition, perception and awareness. On an out-going wavelength, it is that which spurs us toward the communication of those perceptions and awareness.[16]

Astrologers therefore think of Mercury in the birth chart as something that acts as a mediator or negotiator and helps with communication.

Mercury the Messenger God

In myth Mercury is named after the God that the Greeks called Hermes. And Hermes replaced the Babylonian god Nebo and then later the Romans named him Mercurius. This poor God had a number of name changes before it was agreed to call him Mercury.

In the Greek myth soon after being born, Hermes set off in search of the cattle belonging to his brother Apollo. He made their 'hooves go backward, the front ones last and the back ones first' and hid them in the cave of the Sun god Apollo.[6]

He is also known as the trickster God because of all the naughty things he got up to.

Hermes was also the only God capable of travel to the deadly Hades underworld and back again. This is similar to the reality of the planet's surface temperatures being so extreme: hot/cold.

Mercury is now depicted as a God with winged feet, travelling great distances at lightning speeds as the messenger of the gods. It is these attributes that we mirror in Astrology. We're not saying that the attributes are exactly the same as the planet Mercury, just that they're comparable.

That they have similar qualities.

Mercury has a dark and light side.
Sometimes communication can be bright and breezy and other times dark and moody.

Our Example Charts

In our example charts, Elizabeth has her Mercury in the sign of Pisces and Robert has his in the sign of Taurus.

This is a great combination as Water and Earth get along nicely.

There's a slightly different combination in the charts of John Lennon and Yoko Ono.

He had Mercury in Scorpio.

She has Mercury in Pisces.

Even though they were both Air Sun signs, both their Mercurys were in Water signs so they communicated with each other in a more sensitive, emotional way.

Your Mercury's Element

Now don't panic, it's not the end of the world if your partner doesn't have a compatible Mercury to you, but it certainly will help your relationship if you pay attention to what sign it is in, and communicate accordingly.

Fire signs need to communicate swiftly and without too much thought. They'll blast you with what they want, and expect, and at the very least will reply with a Yes, or a No.

Air signs just need to feel heard and understood. They don't need agreement, or even sympathy, just an acknowledgement of their views or opinions.

Earth signs need time to process requests or thoughts. Certainly don't rush an earth sign Mercury, you'll only flummox them!

Water sign Mercurys feel better when the emotional component of that they're saying is accepted.

In my first husband's case, we did have a Mercury problem. He has Mercury in Gemini and I've got mine in Pisces. He's Air, I'm Water and all that resulted in... was fog!

We were together for 10 years, so it wasn't that bad, but I sometimes felt as if he didn't understand how I *felt,* which is very important for someone with a Water sign Mercury.

So before you make a judgement about your relationship, having taken into account your Ascendants, Suns, Moons, Chart Shape, Venus and Mars and you're still having difficulties, have a think about your Mercurys.

Who is talking, and who is listening.

Letter from an Astrologer

'Dear Mary, I have never written to another astrologer before, but I truly believe you are gifted by God, and felt compelled to thank you. I am a 45-year-old astrologer and herbalist born and living in USA. I recently met a man, my "soul-mate", based on composite charts with all of the best aspects indicating friendship, love, sex, and marriage.

When we met, the chemistry was true to our charts, he courted me and was the first to say out loud he wanted to grow old with me. Ironically, he doesn't believe in Astrology because he's a Christian-First Baptist.

Then suddenly and unexpectedly, less than 24 hours after leaving me a voice mail that he misses me and loves me, he sent me an email that he wasn't ready to get married...right now and didn't know when he would be.

I've been racking my brain analysing transits, progressions, etc. and even looked to Chinese and Hindu Astrology as well. I was at the point of mental and physical exhaustion researching whether or not I should wait for him. Tonight I accidentally came across your site and read: "When someone isn't ready to commit, the simple truth is–they don't love you."

I have helped so many people in my life, it's truly amazing how God sent you to me exactly when I needed you, with exactly what I needed–which is the premise of your work and why I believe you are gifted by God. Because our charts were so perfect I couldn't let go and would have wasted the rest of my life waiting and hoping. Thank you for setting me free with your simple profound words of wisdom.
Respectfully,'
M***** Astrologer/Herbalist USA

The above email is an example of what can happen when Astrologers – and people who are interested in Astrology – lose all sense of groundedness when love strikes. No matter how wonderful your charts might look together you must make sure you allow your relationship to reveal its true nature.

Unrequited Love and Astrology
One thing that (mostly) ladies ask me a lot is: 'Am I compatible with Mr X?'

Now, even people that know nothing about Astrology somehow know, maybe it's because of magazine articles, that Astrology will give them some insight into the sort of people who will make them a good partner.
This is perfectly true.

Astrology will highlight aspects of your chart and your beloved's that are good.

However, what Astrology won't do, is 'tell you' or indicate, or suggest if that person you're thinking of falling in love with has also fallen in love with you!

Compatibility

I have written about this before.

About a lady who was absolutely, 100% convinced that the man who would be her soul-mate was: Michael Jackson.

And considering this particular lady lived in Iceland, thousands of miles away from Mr Jackson in the USA, and she had no intention of packing up and leaving Iceland, I was at a loss to understand how she thought she'd be able to make a relationship from this 100% compatibility.

Don't let this happen to you!!

In fact, if you're dating someone right now do NOT ask me if you're compatible until at least 3 months into your relationship.

You might be 100% compatible with Mr/Miss/Ms Right but she might leave the lid off the toothpaste, or kiss her dog, or have terrible relatives, or he might snore, or lie in when you're raring to go. Or the new love of your life might like lots of spices in their food and you don't. There are plenty of reasons to NOT get along with someone, so please curb your urge to find out your compatibility.

When They Don't Love You Back

Now, in affairs of love, the worst-case scenario is when you love someone, madly, deeply and completely... and they don't love you back.

At first, they might be polite and answer your texts, or calls or say 'Hello' to you at work or on the bus or in the pub but that doesn't makes them fancy you.

They might even talk with you, or laugh at your jokes, or even kiss you, but that still doesn't mean they're in love with you.

They might even sleep with you, borrow money from you, take your child/ren to school, make their breakfasts, but still, they might not love you.

A long time ago I did a phone reading for lady who loved someone she worked with. She'd made a stuffed doll of this man (!) and wanted to know if it was a good idea for her to send this doll to the man of her dreams.

I very firmly told her it was *not*.

When someone is in a bad way, and 'madly' in love that isn't reciprocated, being gentle or subtle does *not* work. It takes a lot of effort and energy to convince someone that the person they're 'madly' in love with, doesn't love them back.

The love object might have already dropped lots of subtle hints and the loved-up person is so busy 'being madly in love' that they haven't picked up all these subtle cues.

I've had clients write their love object letters, emails, send them presents (this happens a lot), buy them/or cook them meals, buy them clothes, put them up, take them 'under their wing', text them incessantly, Facebook post them, tweet them (doesn't happen too much) Instant-gram them, bombard them with social media messages until the love object goes into hiding.

Obsessional Messages

Imagine for a minute, someone you *really* don't like bombarding you with affectionate and obsessional messages and communications.

Imagine how you would feel.

You certainly wouldn't want to date them, love them or sleep with them. In fact some men *do* sleep with obsessed women in the faint and desperate hope that the Loved-Up-Person will then leave them alone.

Then the bargaining starts.

If only I can invite him/her over for lunch, if only I can see him/her for just a drink, or a film, or even a talk, or a chat... and the obsession grows like a sort of Hungry Ghost, eating everything in its way. Astrologically the sort of people who are more likely to do this are people with Pluto near the Ascendant, or conjunct the Sun or Moon, or in the 1st or 12th houses. I really recommend if this is you, to read Donna Cunningham's *Healing Pluto Problems*.

No other book comes near hers for very practical advice.

Now, don't think for one minute I'm only telling you this because I'm a therapist. I'm explaining what happens from a place of personal experience and I know exactly what happens, so really this is written to help you, because it once happened to me and I know what it's like.

I have noticed it's worse for female clients who have lost their fathers, or in men who have lost their mothers when young. That death brings a deep sense of loss that can only occur from such a personal relationship. The grief of losing that parent has never truly been healed, and the Hungry Ghost of Love eats their energy and makes matters much, much worse.

Have a think about your life. Have you lost someone? Has someone died that you loved and you thought you'd never replace that love? Get some help and find ways to safely heal that loss within you. Take your time. Be kind to yourself. Remember you're not alone.

So, how do you know if someone *does* love you?

When They Do Love You Back
You'll know because they'll tell you.
They'll text and say it.
Email and say it.
Say it to your face.
They'll write you letters, doodle your name, make 'sticky notes' about you, put random pictures on your notice board or car windscreen and write how much they love that person in the photo... and more.

They'll be happy to see you happy and sad when you're sad and try to alleviate your suffering. They wouldn't want for one minute to see you in pain or upset and certainly wouldn't like to think they have ever caused you any grief.

Being loved is a simple, generous feeling.
There is no struggle. It just feels right.

So let's discuss a few more issues that might prevent you from living in a state of loving bliss.

When He/She is Married

Dear me.
This happens *a lot*.
I see so many clients who have fallen in love with someone who is already in a relationship. Not only in a relationship but legally married! Sometimes with children in the mix.

Gemini, Sagittarius and Pisces are the 'worst' offenders, but it can happen to any sign.
And then there is the ménage a trois. The threesome. This causes untold amounts of suffering for all involved.

Mr and Mrs Perfect are married and they have 2 or 3 children. Then Mrs. Perfect feels as if all the glamour and love has gone out of the relationship.
Or Mr. Perfect thinks Mrs. Perfect doesn't give him the same attention she did when they first met and thinks she is 'giving' too much to the children and he wanders off, or is nabbed by someone who sees the cracks in the façade.

Untold amounts of anxiety and upsetment are created.

What we're going to do is outline some of the general problems I come across.

As yet I've never read for anyone who was having an affair, is female, the man is married and he successfully leaves his wife (and children) and settles down and marries the woman he is having an affair with.

Why?

Because the affair isn't real life. It's a smokescreen.

What generally happens is the chappie who is having the affair *does* leave his wife, but soon afterwards finds someone new.

Not the person he had the affair with.

Don't ask me why that happens. I'm not too sure. It's as if the affair confirms the marriage is not working but when the home/wife and children are lost, the 'reward' of the affair-lady just isn't strong enough. Now there is nothing to keep concealed, nothing to fantasise about. Nothing. When there was nothing to begin with other than the Breaking-The-Rules thing, now that nothingness doesn't satisfy any more.
A bit like eating far too much chocolate. Eventually you never want to touch a bar again... until the next time.

Are You Living in the Past or Worrying About the Future?

I must confess I'm a big fan of Eckhart Tolle. That's not his real name, he changed it before he was published but his book *The Power of Now* has some very useful and enlightening information about how to live a more peaceful, happy life.
He's an Aquarius = New Thinker with Moon in Taurus = Practical.

One point he makes in his book is:
'Unease, anxiety, tension, stress, worry ~ all forms of fear ~ are caused by too much future, and not enough presence.
Guilt, regret, resentment, grievances, sadness, bitterness, and all forms of non-forgiveness are caused by too much past, and not enough presence.'

When we get stuck in the past: *'He did that, she did/said that'* all adds to our own grief. Someone can't make you unhappy, only if you let him or her.

When we worry about the future: *'I need a different job/salary/house/partner'* then we also add to our own stresses.

If we can evaluate each day we are with our partner as a New Day, then we might be a lot more contented. The thoughts that run through people's minds in a few hours is staggering.
I know.
I've tracked mine.

Thoughts such as: *'Will he/she think this or that about my hair/coat/shoes?'* or *'Should I start writing again today or will it be too noisy?'* or *'Hmph, the milk isn't in the fridge and I told him that we were getting low, didn't he get the hint?'*...

On and on this little non-stop rattle of thoughts will make me feel bad/sad/low/angry/upset etc.

I set myself a task one day to 'watch' my thoughts. It does take a bit of practice, but nevertheless it's very interesting. I watched them worry about so many seemingly unimportant things, that had you asked me if I was worrying about them, I would have immediately said 'No!'

Don't be a slave to your thoughts. Get to know them. Eckhart says they're the ego talking. And to be happier, we need to express our deeper, inner self, not the ego bits that need lots of attention.
You could say Astrologically that the Sun is the Ego and The Moon is the deeper-feeling self. So get to know yours and make peace with it.

Anyway, living in the past, blaming your partner for this, that and the other won't make him or her happier, or you for that matter.
Worrying about the future also makes happiness a lot less likely.
Obviously, plan for the future, but don't live there permanently in your mind.

The Home Improvement Committee
& The Mr Fix-It Club

I know women who join what John Gray, author of
Men are from Mars and Women are from Venus,
calls The Home Improvement Committee when they
start a relationship.

They meet a man who is unemployed, or working in a
job that she feels *'isn't good enough'* and before you
know it, she's signed him up for a University degree,
bought him a suit and is locking him in the spare
room to complete his assignments.

She can see his 'potential' and instead of accepting
him as he is, which she did when they first met, she
believes she can make him *even better* when he does
or attains certain things.

She treats her man like he is something that can be
'improved'.

Needless to say, it never works...

Men join another club called the Fix-It Club and
whenever their partner seems down, or unhappy or
sad, he tries to 'fix' her by making lots of suggestions.

Women don't need to be fixed! They're not broken
cars! They need time to talk about their feelings. And
also their fears, or worries. Women do feel better
being able to talk about things. And men, as a general
rule, feel worse.

Men prefer to 'do' stuff.

When I see a man for a reading, no matter what is
going on in his life, he wants to know what to 'do'
about it.

Once a woman has had the time and space to talk
about where she's at and what's going on, generally,
she will formulate a plan and feel better

Chapter Eight

Further Loving Tactics

Sometimes when things aren't going how you want them to, all you want to do is find out how to help yourself feel better. This segment offers some suggestions.

The Bach Flower Remedies

In 1933 Dr Edward Bach, a medical doctor and Homeopath published a little booklet called *The Twelve Healers and Other Remedies.* His theory was that if the emotional component a person was suffering from was removed, their life would be far happier.

I tend to agree with this kind of thinking, as most worries and problems, if not addressed, will only get bigger, not smaller.

Removing the emotional issue and bringing a bit of stability into your life, when you are having a hard time, can improve your overall sense of contentment with any situation you might be in.

Knowing which Bach Flower Essence can help certain worries and upsetments gives you more control over your life. I recommend the essences a lot in my practice if I feel a certain part of a person's chart is under stress... and usually it's the Moon that needs help.

The essences describe the negative aspects of the character, which are focused on during treatment. This awareness helps reverse those trends, so when our emotional selves are nice and comfortable, we can then face each day with more strength.

I've quoted Dr Bach's actual words for each sign.[17]

Remember to seek medical attention if symptoms don't get better and/or seek professional counselling.

Aries Moon
Bach Flower Essence Impatiens.
'Those who are quick in thought and action and who wish all things to be done without hesitation or delay.'

Taurus Moon
Bach Flower Essence Gentian.
'Those who are easily discouraged. They may be progressing well in the affairs of their daily life, but any small delay or hindrance to progress causes doubt and soon disheartens them.'

Gemini Moon
Bach Flower Essence Cerato.
'Those who have not sufficient confidence in themselves to make their own decisions.'

Cancer Moon
Bach Flower Essence Clematis.
'Living in the hopes of happier times, when their ideals may come true.'

Leo Moon
Bach Flower Essence Vervain.
'Those with fixed principles and ideas, which they are confident are right.'

Virgo Moon
Bach Flower Essence Centuary.
'Their good nature leads them to do more than their own share of work and they may neglect their own mission in life.'

Libra Moon
Bach Flower Essence Scleranthus.
'Those who suffer from being unable to decide between two things, first one seeming right then the other.'

Scorpio Moon
Bach Flower Essence Chicory.
'They are continually correcting what they consider wrong and enjoy doing so.'

Sagittarius Moon
Bach Flower Essence Agrimony.
'They hide their cares behind their humor and jesting and try to bear their trials with cheerfulness.'

Capricorn Moon
Bach Flower Essence Mimulus.
'Fear of wordly things, illness, pain, accident, poverty, of dark, of being alone, of misfortune. They secretly bear their dread and do not speak freely of it to others'

Aquarius Moon
Bach Flower Essence Water Violet.
'For those who like to be alone, very independent, capable and self-reliant. They are aloof and go their own way.'

Pisces Moon
Bach Flower Essence Rock Rose
'For cases where there even appears no hope or when the person is very frightened or terrified.'

The best way to use the essences is to take two drops from the stock bottle and put them into a glass of water and sip. I tend to recommend putting them into a small water bottle, and sipping them throughout the day, at least four times.

Homeopathic Remedies

While the Bach Flower Remedies can help with your Moon sign's struggles, homeopathic remedies can help reduce mental worries.
Just like the flower essences, they're easy to take, cheap to buy, don't have side-effects, are non-addictive and are available on-line and in most health food stores.

Arsenicum

If you're worrying, pacing up and down, not able to sleep and sick with all the worry, Arsenicum helps.

People who need Arsenicum album usually have a range of symptoms that are characterised by anxiety, panic attacks and obsessive behaviour. Physically, they are often extremely lacking in energy. They may feel very restless and are frequently sensitive to cold. Typically, people are worse at night, and insomnia is also a common complaint.

Grief and Sadness

These next two remedies highlight the importance of grief and sadness as major triggers of depression and anxiety, along with feelings of abandonment. Natrum Muriaticum (salt) and Ignatia are the remedies most prescribed for this and ones I use in my private practice quite a lot as they're so helpful.

Natrum Muriaticum

The key characteristics of Natrum Muriaticum (also called Nat Mur) include emotional vulnerability, sensitivity to music, avoidance of any risk of being hurt, a tendency to dwell too much on the past, and ailments connected to feelings of grief. Nat Mur also helps best if the grief you're suffering is from a long time ago and something has just recently triggered it.

I expect this would have been a fabulous remedy for Elizabeth Barrett to have taken when she was still suffering from the death of her brother and mother.

I used this remedy a lot when I worked in a drugs detox centre as so many of the clients had sad experiences in their childhoods. A key characteristic of people needing this remedy is they feel worse when they're consoled and feel better on their own to cry in private. They are the epitome of the typical 'stiff upper lip' that is so prevalent in UK society. Saying they feel alright, when they're obviously not.

Ignatia

Ignatia has key signs including emotional sensitivity, a habit of sighing and conflicts between feelings and reality. These are people who are mentally and physically exhausted by long concentrated grief. They've been badly affected by anger, grief or disappointed love and can brood in solitude over imaginary troubles.

They are very, very emotional, impatient and easily offended.

If you're so tearful you can barely think straight, Ignatia will help you face the day without breaking down every second. It will bring you a deep sense of calm.

Aconite

If you're really scared your relationship is going to end then please use Aconite.
This is the ideal remedy for mental anxiety, worry and extreme fear.
People that need this remedy are restless, anxious and do everything really speedily. They're startled easily and will jump at sudden noises. They're constantly on edge. Using this remedy, especially if symptoms come on suddenly, will bring peace of mind.

Hypnotherapy

The easiest way to describe hypnotherapy is to say that it helps the mind relax. And as we've already discussed, having a relaxed mind will help you deal with any problems more easily.
I have made two hypno tracks for the readers of this book.

One is to help you find your Soul Mate, the other is to help you get in touch with your Inner Wise Self.

You can download them FREE on these links:

www.maryenglish.com/AttractingYourSoulMate.mp3

www.maryenglish.com/YourWiseSelf.MP3

Thank you

I hope you have benefited from reading this book and now feel a little more confident about your love life. If you'd like to learn more about Astrology, do check out my FREE Podcast http://astromary.libsyn.com/

If you've enjoyed reading this or feel my words have been helpful in any way, I would love it if you would tell others about your experience. Authors make their living from the sales of their books and E-books. And the only way a book can benefit people is when the reader gives feedback to other potential readers. A review on Amazon will really help spread the word that Astrology is a wonderful way to Help You Love Better. And your review will make my day:) xx

Thank you
In Peace
Mary
www.maryenglish.com

References
Introduction
Sonnets from the Portuguese by Elizabeth Barrett Browning with illustrations by Margaret Armstrong, 1902, New York, GP Putnam's Sons
https://archive.org/stream/sonnetsfromportu00brow#page/n95/mode/2up

Chapter One
1. Marc Edmund Jones, *The Guide to Horoscope Interpretation*, Quest Edition, 1972 Theosophical Publishing House, Illinois, USA.
2. Mary English, *The Astrology of Indigos, Everyday Solutions to Spiritual Difficulties*, Hensley Healing Publishing, 2013
3. http://www.browningsociety.org/ebb.html

Whole Sign House System
http://www.arhatmedia.com/whole_sign.html

Chapter Two
4/5. Paul Sutherland, *Astronomy: A Beginner's Guide to the Sky at Night*, Igloo Books, Sywell, Northampton, 2007
6. Clare Gibson, *The Astronomy Handbook: Guide to the Night Sky,* Parkham Books, Devon, 2009
7.
https://www.citizensadvice.org.uk/relationships/living-together-marriage-and-civil-partnership/living-together-and-marriage-legal-differences/
8. http://www.unmarried.org/common-law-marriage-fact-sheet

Chapter Four

9. https://www.poetryfoundation.org/poems-and-poets/poems/detail/43769
and *The Love Poems of Elizabeth and Robert Browning*, foreword by Louis Untermeyer,
Barnes & Noble Books, New York, 1994
N.B. the word 'dartles' is not a typo. It means to move back and forth
10. https://www.theguardian.com/society/2004/jun/21/childrensservices.uknews
11. Dr Lisa Doodson, *How to be a Happy Stepmum*, Vermilion, 2010
12. https://fnf.org.uk/

Chapter Five

13. V. E. Stack, *The Love Letters of Robert Browning and Elizabeth Barrett*, Century, an imprint of Century Hutchinson Ltd, London WC2N 4NW, 1969

Chapter Six

14. Yoko Ono Quote
http://www.thedailybeast.com/articles/2015/10/13/yoko-ono-i-still-fear-lennon-s-killer.html

Chapter Seven

15. Clare Gibson, *The Handbook of Astronomy*, Kerswell Books Ltd, 2009
16. Christine Rose, *Astrological Counselling, A basic guide to astrological themes in person to person relationships,* The Aquarian Press, Northamptonshire, 1982
Eckhart Tolle, *The Power of NOW, A Guide to Spiritual Enlightenment,* Hodder & Stoughton Ltd, 338 Euston Road, London NW1 3BH, 2011

Chapter Eight

17. Edward Bach, *The Twelve Healers and Other Remedies,* 26th impression, The C.W. Daniel Company Ltd, Essex, England, 1996

Bibliography

Stephen Arroyo, *Person-to-Person Astrology – Energy Factors in Love, Sex & Compatibility,* Frog Ltd, Berkeley, California, 2007.

Mary Coleman, *Picking Your Perfect Partner Through Astrology, A Guide to Compatibility in Relationships,* CRCS Publications, Post Office Box 1460, Sebastopol, California 95473, USA, 1996.

Rose Murray, *When Will You Marry? Your Romantic Destiny Through Astrology,* Llewellyn Publications, P.O. 64383, St. Paul, MN 551640-0383,1995.

Christopher McIntosh, *Astrology, The Stars and Human Life: A Modern Guide*, Macdonald Unit 75, St. Giles House, 49 Poland Street, London W.1, 1970.

Christopher McIntosh, *The Astrologers and Their Creed, An Historical Outline,* Arrow Books Ltd, 3 Fitzroy Square, London W1, 1971.

Rae Orion, *Astrology for Dummies,* IDG Books Worldwide, Inc, 919 E. Hillsdale Blvd, Suite 400, Foster City, CA 94494, 1999.

Edited by V.E. Stack, *The Century Lives & Letters, The Love Letters of Robert Browning & Elizabeth Barrett,* Century Hutchinson Ltd, Brookmount House, 62-65 Chandos Place, London WC2N 4NW, 1987.

Edited by Louis Untermeyer, *The Love Poems of Elizabeth and Robert Browning,* Barnes & Noble, Inc, New York, 1994.

Edited by Stanley Appelbaum, *Sonnets from the Portuguese and Other Poems by Elizabeth Barrett Browning,* Dover Publications, Inc, 31 East 2nd Street, Mineola, N.Y. 11501, 1992.

Further Reading

Donna Cunningham, *Healing Pluto Problems,* Samuel Weiser Inc, P.O. Box 612, York beach, ME, 1986; also available as a Kindle E-Book on Amazon.

Judy Hall, *Hands Across Time: The Soulmate Enigma,* Findhorn Press 1997

Further Information

The Astrological Association of Great Britain was founded in June 1958 in London. No matter what your level of experience, whether student or teacher, amateur or professional, or whether your approach to astrology is traditional or modern, scientific or spiritual, the AA has a place for you.
www.astrologicalassociation.com

21460513R00087

Printed in Poland
by Amazon Fulfillment
Poland Sp. z o.o., Wrocław